METADATA ESSENTIALS

Proven Techniques for Book Marketing and Discovery

Written by Jake Handy and Margaret Harrison

GRAPHIC ARTS
BOOKS®

ISBN: 9781513260891 (paperback)
ISBN: 9781513260907 (hardbound)
ISBN: 9781513260914 (e-book)

Graphics: Check Mark by REVA, check list by unlimicon, Shopping Cart by Adrien Coquet,
and bars graph by Mourad Mokrane from the Noun Project.

Printed in the U.S.A.

Edited by Jess Johns
Indexed by Sam Arnold-Boyd

Published by Graphic Arts Books

GRAPHIC ARTS
BOOKS®

GraphicArtsBooks.com

Proudly distributed by Ingram Publisher Services.

GRAPHIC ARTS BOOKS
Publishing Director: Jennifer Newens
Marketing Manager: Angela Zbornik
Editor: Olivia Ngai
Design & Production: Rachel Lopez Metzger

With gratitude to Lindsey Collier who contributed to this book.

CONTENTS

INTRODUCTION

Metadata: What's It All About?

Whether you're an author or a publisher, **metadata**—that is, the data that describes and differentiates your book—should be one of your biggest considerations. It's of huge importance to your customers because it brings a book to life for the buyer and provides important details on what he or she should expect. Titles with incomplete or nonspecific metadata result in higher returns and, generally, lower sales.[1]

Supplying metadata might seem like an easy problem to tackle, but it's been incredibly difficult for authors and publishers to know where they should focus their efforts. Spreadsheets and "best practices" documents place a heavy emphasis on what can be sent throughout the supply chain. But what metadata should you send? What's most important?

Through extensive research, surveying, and interviewing, we've gathered many insights to share with you on what metadata matters most. The fact is that many publishers are wasting time on metadata that may never see the light of day, let alone contribute to sales growth. We wrote this book to help publishers and authors prioritize their metadata efforts and to demystify the way that booksellers, discovery sites, search engines, and libraries catalog, market, and merchandise your book.

In the pages that follow, you'll find tons of unique research, screenshots, and case studies to give you the tools you need to better prioritize the time, money and effort you spend on metadata.

1 The Nielsen Company. "Nielsen Book US Study: The Importance of Metadata for Discoverability and Sales". Survey. December 31 2016.

FIGURE 1. *Metadata in the book industry. Unfortunately, many publishers waste a lot of time on metadata that no one will ever use!*

Metadata for Books: The Current Landscape

One of the keys to knowing what metadata to send about a product lies in figuring out the best way to transmit all that information from your system directly to the consumer. Since publishers, aggregators, distributors, and retailers ingest and distribute data, and each party has its own way of interpreting the data, it's easy to see how things can get complicated.

Before the XML metadata standard ONIX was introduced in 2000, publishers would send all their metadata in spreadsheet format. However, since there weren't (and, to a large extent, still aren't) metadata formatting standards across the publishing industry, it was very time consuming to reformat individualized data for multiple trading partners who accepted the data in different ways.

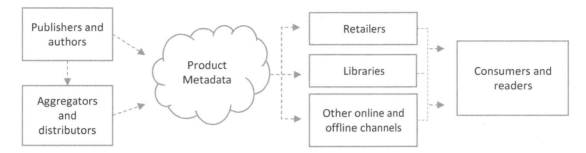

FIGURE 2. *Product metadata proliferates across channels and across the Web, to online retailers, search engines, and websites, as well as physical bookstore and library shelves and categories—all the places where consumers ultimately find and buy books.*

While some publishers currently send metadata in a spreadsheet format, each data recipient has its own unique template. However, an ever-growing number of publishers, aggregators, distributors, and retailers are utilizing ONIX to help standardize the transmission of data.

The existing standards we will discuss in this book primarily center around ONIX, which is the XML standard for transmitting all types of book data, including metadata. It's important to understand how each metadata element we define and describe here can be added to any standard ONIX 3.0 XML feed. It's also important to note that this book is not meant to clearly explain the intricacies of ONIX or its proper usage, but to explain how the elements listed within can be referenced in existing ONIX codelists to achieve beautiful, concise metadata. For further information about ONIX 3.0, please visit the official website (editeur.org/83/Overview/).

Knowledge or use of ONIX is not a requirement to benefit from this collection of metadata essentials. Each element discussed can be utilized in other standards or even in a custom XML feed. All the tips and tricks we will talk about are on the content level, more related to what your metadata looks like and less to how it is delivered or communicated through a catalogue or distribution system.

While the majority of the industry is rooted in ONIX, the standardization for the metadata content within varies from publisher to publisher, library to library, and so on.

An interesting parallel in terms of standards can be found in the music industry. iTunes, the leading channel for music sales and subscriptions, requires a bare minimum of genre, track title, artist name, and album title. There is movement within certain musical genres, such as Classical, for artists to provide much more information. That being said, each distribution pillar in the music industry has made little effort to truly expand into enhanced metadata where it might be desirable.

Similarly, within the book industry there is a recognized bare minimum by most distribution channels that always includes the basics. Within certain subjects—again, similar to Classical music in the above example—there is a desire to provide more details, such as an emphasis on contributor biographies. On the whole, however, the standards tend to focus on the minimum and let enhanced metadata either fall off completely or come in a sloppy, unorganized manner. This was fantastic news 10 years ago, since it meant that authors of all walks of life were able to submit their books to stores in no time. In the current crowded market, though, where social media advertising and metadata intelligence are key to maximizing sales, the lack of standardization for elements of enhanced metadata is a liability.

Why Metadata Matters

The modern consumer wants to be engaged. Giving a reader an accurate preview of the content through your metadata is the key to hooking them to your products. **When a reader lands at your book's page on the Kindle Store or elsewhere, they want to see as much information as possible. This mimics readers walking up and down book store and library rows for hours, scanning the pages of books, seeking out their favorite contributors, eyeing the art, and selecting the book that interests them the most. Offering them more information up front will always lead to more opportunities to hook them.**

This is the key to the metadata essentials outlined in this book. There are multitudes of real, tangible data points that publishers, librarians, and retailers alike are not utilizing to the best of their ability. From simple elements like product type and title to the deep complexities of contributor data, keywords, and subject codes, every piece of metadata that accompanies your book serves an important role in boosting discoverability and sales.

SEO: What You Need to Know

Metadata and discoverability go hand in hand, especially when it comes to selling content online. Some publishers and authors have begun to explore how metadata can improve the ranking of their books in search results. This practice, called search engine optimization or SEO, is a trending topic in the book industry, and for good reason. More than a fad, **SEO** is an important consideration for publishers and authors who want to see their books surface to the most relevant customers.

Wondering how to get started with SEO or looking for some tips? Read on! We'll give you all the tips you need in the next chapter.

CHAPTER 1: How Books are Discovered

Search engine optimization is critical to success in today's market, and metadata is the key to making your book discoverable to consumers. In this chapter, we'll help you understand how Amazon's search algorithm works and which metadata elements are essential to help place your book among top search results for relevant queries. We'll also examine the potential for exploiting smart searching at other online bookstores.

Think about how a consumer might have stumbled across a good book in a bookstore or library in the 1990s. If a publisher has paid for advertising, the book might be featured in a bookstore in a display. A bookseller or a librarian might provide a recommendation. A book cover might catch the eye of a discerning browser, prompting that reader to pick up the book, inspect the back cover and jacket flaps, and flip through the pages. A reader might go to a particular section or shelf, such as Italian cookbooks, and look for a title of interest, probably based on the title name on the spine of the book.

These discovery experiences still happen today, but consider how limited each experience is. It's limited to the inventory on the shelf, selected by a buyer or librarian. It's limited to the knowledge of my bookseller or librarian. It's limited to the publishers who have advertising budgets.

Enter search engine optimization. The internet has opened a floodgate of opportunity for authors and publishers through the ability to enable long-tail discovery. True, you'll still compete against ad dollars, online and in-store, and you'll compete against well-known brands. But you're no longer limited by the knowledge or budget of a bookseller or librarian. By ensuring your book can be returned in the top search results of relevant online queries, you can connect with more readers than you ever imagined. This takes some practice. It also requires an understanding of how search engines work.

Note: Because this is a book about metadata, we focus on the role that metadata plays in Amazon search results and at other bookstores and libraries. SEO is a much broader topic, and you may have some interest in optimizing your website for Google search results, but we won't cover that in depth here in this book, though by following our guidelines you may find that your product detail pages at retailers and on your own site achieve better rankings at Google and other online search engines. For more on general website optimization, we recommend you start with an SEO resource like Moz (moz.com) where you'll find a robust and broad SEO toolkit for site content optimization.

During the rest of this chapter, and throughout the book, we'll focus on optimizing the search results of your books on retail, library, and other discovery websites. Because these are product-driven searches (generally, people go to retail sites because they want to buy something), rather than question-driven (generally, people perform online searches to have a question answered, which may or may not be product-driven), the search journey is somewhat different.

Not all search engines are created equal. As you'll learn, Amazon is the most sophisticated retail search engine by far, but it's important to understand how search engines contribute to the book-discovery process across the book landscape so you can improve the odds of your title coming up in every relevant search, whether at Amazon, Booktopia in Australia, or OverDrive for library patrons.

How Amazon Search Works

Amazon's search algorithm is called A9. As we've observed, unlike Google's search algorithms, designed to provide the most accurate answer to your question, Amazon is singularly focused on getting you to buy as much as possible on the site. To achieve this, Amazon has designed A9 to call up the products that are relevant to you and also the products you are most likely to buy. Accordingly, key factors in Amazon search include:

- Click-through rate (CTR), measured by how often a consumer clicks through to a product page from search results
- Conversion rate, measured by how often a consumer who visits the product page actually purchases the product

- Overall sales, based on gross and net revenue to Amazon
- Keyword relevance, measured by the degree a product matches a search for a keyword

A unique and specific book title, such as *The Hidden Life of Trees*, will have better search relevance than a less unique book title, such as *The Nest*, which will share search results with other nonbook products.

FIGURE 3. *Search results for* The Nest *at Amazon.com, captured December 2017.*

There are many factors that contribute to search results at Amazon. It's important to remember that an algorithm is a melting pot of all those factors, so you won't always see a direct cause-and-effect outcome to changing your metadata for Amazon SEO. By familiarizing yourself with the various factors and search "markers," you can give yourself the best odds of boosting your search results and sales.

For books, Amazon typically matches keyword search to title name first, followed by contributor and subtitle. But there are other factors as well, especially in a more congested search. Remember that Amazon is trying to make the most revenue possible—not just short-term, but long-term—*and* they want you to buy and be satisfied with your purchase so you'll come back. In no particular order, here are other search factors at Amazon:

- **Star reviews.** Positive star ratings (4 or more stars) from Amazon customers are a search marker.

- **Images.** A high-resolution cover (at least 300 dpi and ideally 2560 x 1600 pixels) as well as a back cover and interior images may boost your search results.

- **Bestseller status.** #1 Bestseller status in a particular category at Amazon.

- **Amazon participation.** Participation in Look Inside, Kindle Unlimited and other Amazon programs, including paid ads and exclusivity. Remember, this is only a marker and may not in and of itself contribute to positive search results. You can try nonpaid and nonexclusive options before you go "all in" with an investment or exclusivity.

Metadata for Amazon Search

One of the most important things you can do to boost your SEO at Amazon is to create great metadata that will contribute to click-through rates and conversion rates. You'll find more information on how Amazon uses metadata in Chapter 3 and more details on specific attributes that are important in Chapter 2. If you're reading this book because you are specifically interested in optimizing for Amazon, check out the following sections in Chapter 2 that will make the biggest impact in Amazon search results:

- Titles, Series, and Editions
- Long & Short Descriptions
- Using BISAC & Other Subject Codes the Right Way

- Illustrations & Other Image Details
- Keywords

Beyond Amazon Search & Other Booksellers

You probably weren't surprised to hear that Amazon's search engine is far more sophisticated than any other bookstore. Consider, though, that when it comes to selling books, Amazon can be at a disadvantage: as the online "superstore," Amazon must position books alongside millions of other products in a search, from dishwashers to diapers. A customer browsing for books by a particular phrase (also called a **keyword**) may find other products in search results.

A bookstore or book-focused site has the distinct advantage of focusing on the book-discovery journey. For example, Barnes & Noble has optimized their search engine as well as the web pages that display a book (called **product detail pages**) at bn.com to cater to the many consumers who are searching for particular book series on their site.

A book-focused site may have a landing page for a series or author or even a special promotion, such as a theme or a price promotion. Strand Books, an independent bookstore in New York City, often creates these custom landing pages on their website (strandbooks.com). These landing pages may come up in search results, or a customer searching for a particular author or series may be redirected to the page automatically, depending on the website. Of course, Amazon may do these pages as well, but given that books are merely one of hundreds of categories of other products on the site, they will be more focused on bestsellers and less focused on niche books or local content.

Typically, online booksellers and book websites return search results based on three key metadata elements:

- Title name (depending on the site, this may be a full or partial match)
- Author or contributor
- ISBN or EAN (the unique identifier for your book)

More sophisticated search engines may also **index** (or use as content for search results) the series, subtitle, subject, keywords, format (e.g., hardcover or ebook), or even book descriptions. A small number of book-search engines do factor in star ratings and images, but by and large, most are searching against the title, contributor, and ISBN. This is why, as we'll cover in Chapter 2 and Chapter 3, it's important to create a keyword-rich title, if at all possible. In the wide world of bookselling, it is your best shot at achieving that serendipitous online discovery from a consumer who would otherwise have never heard of your book.

While search beyond Amazon is fairly limited, there are many examples of brilliant bookselling and marketing out there on the web. Here are a few of our favorite examples:

- **Barnes & Noble's Book Graph**. This feature, added to the B&N website during the fall of 2017, displays a map of related books based on metadata and B&N buyer recommendations. This is not the same as the "Customers who bought this product also bought" feature on many online retail sites, which is based on consumer buying behavior. Book Graph is truly based on the subject matter of the book, which may resonate more with book buyers.

- **iBooks & print book searches.** Even though the iBookstore only sells digital books, they index associated print books to ensure a consumer who might be searching

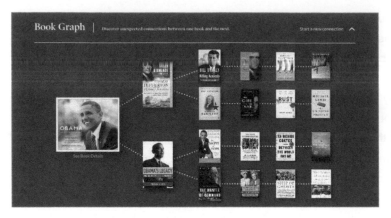

FIGURE 4. *Barnes & Noble Book Graph, launched in 2017, aims to make recommendations based on tastes, not purchase history.*

Google or iBooks with a print ISBN can be connected to the appropriate ebook version. Google Play does this as well. (Read more about how to provide print and ebook ISBNs in your metadata in Chapter 3.)

- **Jet.com and relevance.** We're really impressed by how tight the search results are becoming at Walmart-owned Jet.com. A search for "harry potter and the sorcerer's stone" at most booksellers returns too few results or too many, but Jet.com returned a perfect 14 results, including the illustrated version and a French and Spanish language version, without any fake or irrelevant results.

- **Booktopia and series searches.** Booktopia includes a results summary bar at the top of their search results page with a quick link to refine search based on series, subject, title, or author. For subject and series, the name is shown as a match to allow for easy filtering.

FIGURE 5. *Search results for "slow cooker" at Booktopia.com.au, captured July 2017.*

CHAPTER 2: Take Action!
Metadata Essentials, Your Step-by-Step Guide

Chapter 2 focuses on the nuts and bolts of creating effective metadata, guiding you to the optimal use of every essential element or **attribute**. You'll learn how to write an effective **contributor biography** and **product description**, and we'll explain the importance of precise, search-friendly **BISAC subject codes**. We'll also cover the basics of **HTML markup** here, and we'll demystify **keywords**, **audience code**, **series name**, and much more.

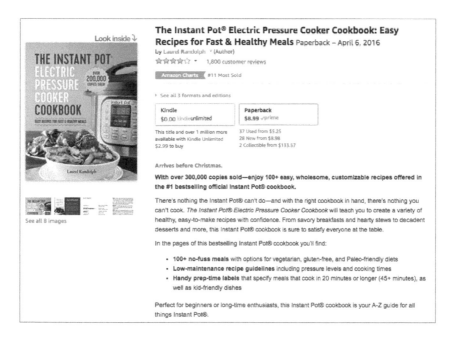

FIGURE 6. *Search results for "slow cooker" at Amazon.com, captured July 2017.*

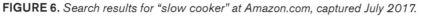

Focus on Metadata that Matters

After reading Chapter 1, you should have a better understanding of why metadata matters for online book discovery. Now we're going to break down each piece of metadata, tell you which are most important, and give you actionable best practices based on our research, interviews, and real-life observations and experiences.

What metadata is really "essential"?

In 2017, we conducted a survey of 60 international booksellers and book discovery partners to better understand how they use metadata elements to inform on-site search and merchandising as well as ordering and stocking decisions.

We then evaluated retailer responses against established SEO best practices and research into how consumers find and buy books to identify the metadata attributes that publishers should focus on to have the greatest impact on book discovery and sales. For each metadata element, we calculated an index score on a scale of 0 to 100 (at right) based on its relevance to retailers, search engines, and consumers, giving heavier weight to those retailers with greater market share. (You can read more about the survey and how specific retailers use metadata in Chapter 3.)

While it is certainly important to have accurate and complete metadata across all of these attributes, we recommend focusing on some key elements to boost discovery and sales of your titles. Ensuring your metadata is intact for these attributes will allow retailers to display the key purchase information consumers crave, as well as equip retail staff to make decisions that will help increase online conversion rates for your titles.

Essentials Index Score

ATTRIBUTE	SCORE
Title	100
Contributor (Author)	100*
Description	97
Series Name	87
Series Number	82
BISAC Subject Code	80
Age Range	80
HTML Markup	74
Related Product	70
Edition Number	70
Territory Rights	69
Product Form (i.e. format)	69
Digital Pre-orders	64
Reading Level	64
Audience Code (e.g. juvenile)	63
BIC or Thema Category	62
Product Form Detail	60
Short Description	57
Contributor Biography	53
Dimensions	52
Illustrations	49
Weight	49
Features	43
Thema Code	37
Keywords	34
BISAC Regional Theme Code	26
Contributor Place	23
International Standard Name Identifier (ISNI)	5

Some respondents only use the first contributor name.

Metadata Checklist

Make sure your book doesn't leave home without:

✓	**Title**	Keep it fewer than 80 characters long, including subtitle, so that it's optimized for mobile.
✓	**Contributor**	Be sure to use all the names from the cover or title page–and be consistent with spellings, middle initials, etc.
✓	**Contributor Bio**	Keep it between 50 and 250 words for each contributor, and avoid using external links such as blogs or author websites–you don't want to drive potential customers away from buying your book!
✓	**Series**	Alert your readers to other titles in a series by including your series name and number, if applicable.
✓	**Description**	Describe your book in a conversational tone, in 200 to 600 words, with a bolded opening line and paragraph breaks (see HTML markup).
✓	**HTML Markup**	In your description, use \<b\> for bold, \<i\> for italics and \<p\> for paragraph breaks, like this: 　　\<b\>\<i\>Metadata is the best!\</i\>\</b\> 　　\<p\>Seriously.\</p\> 　　***Metadata is the best!*** 　　Seriously.
✓	**Genre**	Choose 2 to 3 specific categories (like BISAC subject code) and if you don't find exactly what you need, supplement with keywords.
✓	**Keywords**	Choose 5 to 7 (or more!) or phrases that draw the consumer, and incorporate throughout your metadata–in the description, contributor biography, even title and series;–you can add these keywords plus others in the keyword field, where they will become hidden online search terms.
✓	**Format**	Most specific description of your binding, such as mass market paperback or epub ebook–and be sure to use one ISBN per format to keep formats distinct.
✓	**Review Quotes**	Include 2 to 8 positive review quotes from industry sources, publications, and relevant people such as other authors or reputable bloggers.
✓	**Audience Code**	Make sure your title is merchandised correctly by choosing the appropriate audenice code: general/adult, juvenile (for ages 0–11), or YA (for ages 12–17)–oh, and this should jibe with your genre (that is, use juvenile audience code with juvenile subject codes).
✓	**Age & Grade**	If you choose a juvenile or YA audience code, pick an age range and/or grade range to target; use a two-year age or grade range for children and a four-year age or grade range for YA.

ONIX: A Word to the Wise

If you're not an ONIX user, you can skip this paragraph. Otherwise... psst! Several of the metadata elements detailed within Chapter 2 have various options condensed into numerical codes within ONIX. These elements will be listed first alongside their proper codelist number, like this:

- Product Type (List 150)

Up-to-date documentation and the most current ONIX codelists can be found at http://www.editeur.org/14/Code-Lists/.

TITLES, SERIES & EDITIONS

TITLE

The Title of a book creates the first impression. No matter how good the rest of a book's metadata is, if the title is ambiguous, misleading or too similar to a wide variety of other books, a reader may skip over it as easily as they found it. For this reason, it's important to take time developing a title that both accurately describes your book and avoids any confusion with more popular writings. Titling a book *Lord of the Real Rings* or *The Other Chronicles of Narnia*, outside of any legal implications, will simply bury it under much more established novels that readers already know.

Naming a book similarly to another book in hopes of discovery is an unwise and potentially destructive choice.

There are several requirements to follow to meet the ONIX standard for titles:

- The title within the metadata must match the title on both the cover art and title page.

- Maintain the title's consistency alongside any internal or external identifiers. (ISBN, Publisher Work ID, etc.)

- Include title prefixes and leading articles. (e.g. *The Call of the Wild*, not *Call of the Wild* or *Call of the Wild, The*)

- Omit any subtitle, series, edition, or format information. (These data elements are captured in separate fields.)

- Only use all caps when appropriate for acronyms or stylization.
- A title is required in order to enable a book for pre-order.

Note on ONIX: The title type (List 15) is an ONIX code that can be useful to better identify the title you are delivering or further outline additional titles. This codelist helps to better define the primary title (with things like Title in original language *and* Abbreviated title*) or differentiate any other titles listed alongside the primary* (Alternative title, Expanded title*). Should any additional title be distributed with the primary title, it is vital to use this codelist within the ONIX to clearly define its role.*

SUBTITLE

Following the title is the subtitle. Never include the subtitle within the title ONIX, as these two elements need to be delivered separately regardless of how they are displayed on the cover art or within marketing materials. The subtitle is commonly used to relay further information about the contents of the book. Keep your subtitles accurate and to the point.

A few best practices to follow for subtitles are as follows:

- Use the subtitle to differentiate the book. This is especially helpful for works with otherwise generic titles or with a title similar to other works on the market. (e.g. *The Girls: A Novel*)

- Incorporate important consumer keywords in your subtitle to improve discovery (such as important brands, major characters, themes and topics). (e.g. *Elon Musk: Tesla, SpaceX, and the Quest for a Fantastic Future*)

- Be wary of keyword "stuffing." The subtitle should support search engine optimization and include relevant consumer keywords when possible, but if it's distracting or "spammy" to readers, it will not help convert to sales.

SERIES NAME & NUMBER

Commonly misappropriated within the subtitle, the series name and number is the overarching collection name, and order within it, that a book may belong to. **Just as the subtitle should never be included in the title, the series name and number should never be included in the subtitle.**

The series name is used to specify an ongoing series, and it can be retroactively added should a novel that started as a stand-alone story be bundled into subsequent releases. The series number is not required if order within the series is not meaningful (e.g. an I Can Read! book), but it should be included for books where consumers care about reading order. The series number should only be sent as an integer (1, 2, or 3 versus specifying media types such as Book 1, CD 2, or Narration 3).

Example:
```
    Series Name: Cal Claxton Oregon Mysteries
    Series Number: 5
```

ONIX Example:
```
    <Series>
        <Title>
                <TitleType>01</TitleType>
                <TitleText textcase="02">Cal Claxton Oregon Mysteries</TitleText>
        </Title>
        <NumberWithinSeries>5</NumberWithinSeries>
    </Series>
```

Within ONIX 3.0, the series name and number are defined under collections.

FIGURE 7. *Series data at BN.com, captured December 2017.*

EDITION INFORMATION

A book's edition should never be confused with the series name and number. **The series name and number designate the book's place within a story or release timeline, whereas the edition indicates a book's revision and re-release into an existing or new marketplace.** Editions are differentiated in several ways:

- Substantial changes in content, including revised or additional content. This includes numbered editions of academic and reference works (e.g. *MLA Handbook, 7th Edition*). Typically, at least 20% of the content should be different or new to qualify as a new edition.

- Special packaging or content that is not included with or that is substantively changed from the primary edition of the work. This includes media tie-ins and special editions (e.g. anniversary or signed editions) as well as illustrated, enhanced, annotated, and abridged editions.

- Intended use by a special market. This includes Braille, large print, and teacher and student editions of a work.

Similarly to the series name and number, all elements of an edition should not be included in the book's title or subtitle. Rather, utilize the fields to submit the following elements of editions:

- Edition number
- Edition type
- Edition description

The edition number functions identically to the series number. Always use integers and ensure that the edition number matches what is being relayed in the book's cover art or marketing material.

There are various edition types (List 21) that are outlined in the ONIX codelist. The most important thing to consider when approaching edition types is simple: accuracy. Submitted incorrect edition types can lead to product confusion on multiple levels. You can submit numerous edition types for any one book, as long as they are accurate. Please reference the ONIX codelist for the wide variety of edition types available. There are two specific edition types that should be given special attention:

- Abridged (ABR) or Unabridged (UBR): These must be specified for all audiobooks. Only abridged editions need be specified for physical releases.

- Digital original (DGO): This should be used for any digital releases that are either exclusively digital or were released first digitally.

The edition description should be a short, concise statement that accurately and purposefully combines the edition number and edition type. This is the text information that will be relayed to readers. A good edition description should tell your reader everything they need to know at a quick glance. Although the limit is 100 characters, shooting for around 50 or less is advised. Some examples of well-written edition descriptions include:

- "3rd Edition, completely revised and updated"

- "25th Anniversary Collection Edition"

- "Enhanced edition with video interviews"

CONTRIBUTORS

From the most fundamental contributor role, "author," to more obscure contributor roles like "epilogue by" and "guest editor," the proper acknowledgment of contributors merits close attention.

Contributors are an important part of most digital merchants' strategies to link and relate books to one another. For example, a reader may see a small illustration in a book that they love and wish to explore further. If this artist's contributor metadata is included alongside your book, it allows stores to fine-tune their relational algorithms to lead that reader to book illustrations by the same artists, as well as to illustrations by similar artists—and, in turn, to the authors and other contributors of the books featuring said illustrations.

CORE CONTRIBUTOR DATA

Including more contributor metadata within your book helps create robust, more accurate book metadata throughout the industry, allowing for a fantastic web of information that will place your books in more interested hands. This metadata goes far beyond first name and last name.

METADATA ESSENTIALS
Contributor Data

? THE BASICS
Robust contributor data connects your book to all of the people who helped create it, to all of their other works, and in turn to other similar works.

QUICK TIPS
✓ Include accurate name and role data for all contributors.
✓ Include a brief biography for the primary and other key contributors (e.g. author, co-author, illustrator).
✓ Biographies should be 50 to 150 words long.
✓ Include detail on important places in the contributor's life, their prior works, and affiliations.

ESSENTIALS INDEX

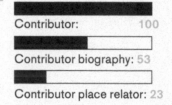

Contributor: 100

Contributor biography: 53

Contributor place relator: 23

🛒 WHAT RETAILERS SAY
▪ **48%** of retailers use contributor bios either onsite for consumers or for internal purposes.
▪ The average accepted word count for a contributor bio is 1,000.

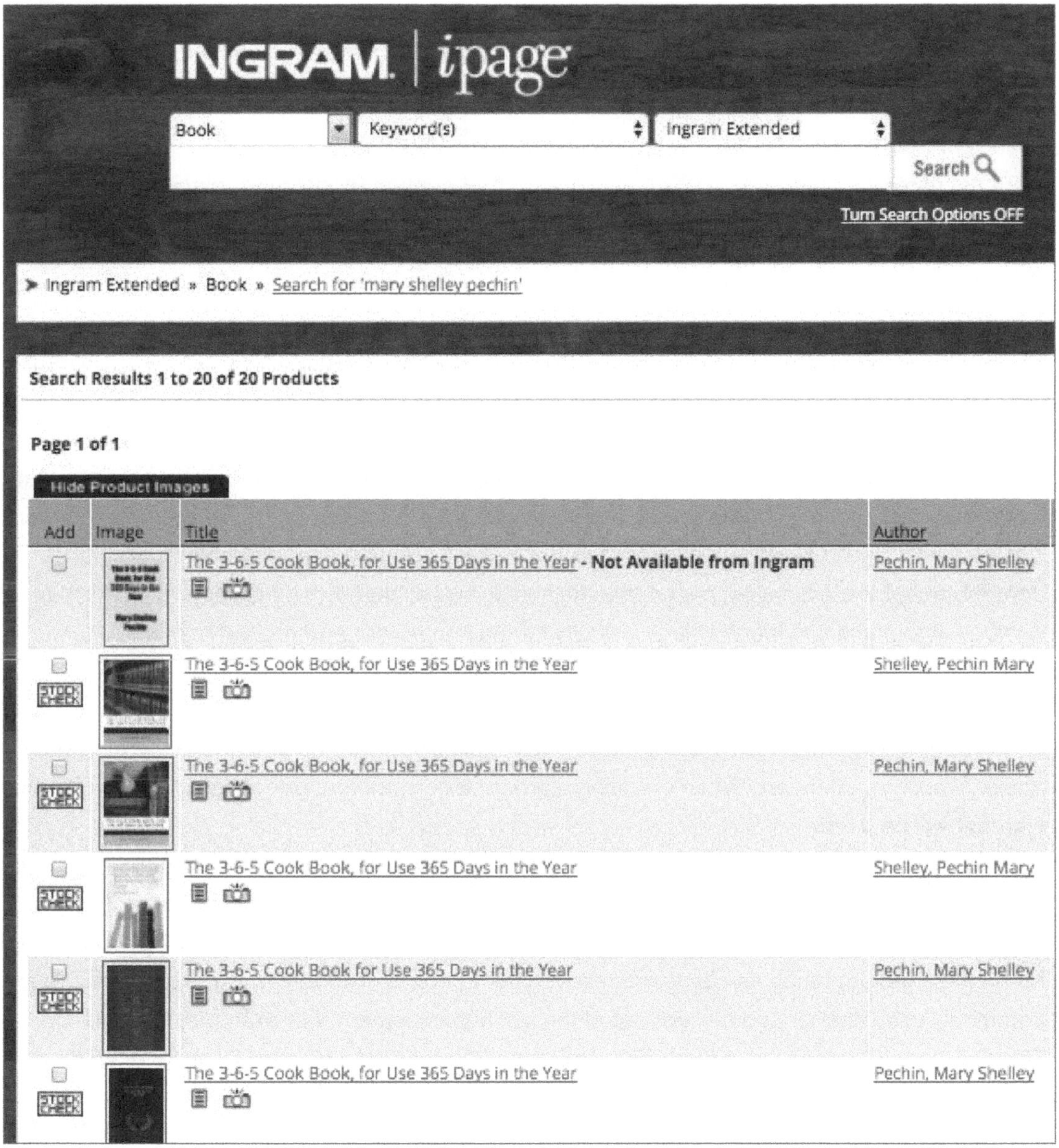

FIGURE 8. *Inconsistent contributor names in Ingram iPage search results, captured December 2017.*

Below are the most important contributor metadata elements that you should always consider for every person involved with a release:

- First name
- Last name
- Name prefixes and titles
- Name suffixes, qualifications, and honors
- Type or role

- Biography
- Location (contributor place relator)
- Prior work by contributor
- Affiliations
- External contributor IDs (including ISNI)

The more contributor metadata you can provide for each unique individual, the better. However, as with other metadata elements, providing information that is incorrect or incomplete leads to metadata that is both useless and harmful to your discoverability. For example, crediting "J.K. Rowling" and "J.K. Roling" (with a missing "w") will create two completely different contributor entries within your own metadata and across all platforms that receive it. This can confuse algorithms and leads to less visibility for the contributor and related books.

CONTRIBUTOR NAME

The **first name** and **last name** elements are self-explanatory but, as outlined in the example above, worthy of attention. When crediting a group or corporation, generally only the last name element will be used.

Name prefixes and titles can be used for both person and organization names, and they must never be included in either the first name or last name elements. For persons, this includes titles such as *Mr.*, *Dr.*, *Sir*, and *Mdme*. These can be communicated in the abbreviated form or spelled out (such as *Doctor* instead of *Dr.*). For organizations, prefixes such as *The* are commonly used and should be kept out of the last name element. For example, when listing *The Pokémon Company* as a publisher, *The* should be recorded as a prefix and *Pokémon Company* as the last name or organization name.

Name suffixes, qualifications, and honors function identically as name prefixes and titles but serve elements that follow the contributor's name rather than precede it. This includes titles such as *Jr.*, *II*, and *PhD*. Organizations generally will not utilize this element.

Note on ONIX: If using ONIX, first name is defined as <NamesBeforeKey> and last name as <KeyNames>. Use the person/organization name type codelist (List 18) to add alternate names such as pseudonyms and earlier known-by names.

Use the unnamed person(s) codelist (List 19) to recognize that a contributor is present but unknown. This includes the option to credit a contributor as anonymous and also provides for unique situations such as:

- *Bundled packaged products containing multiple books, needing to be assigned a "various authors" contributor.*
- *Synthesized voices developed for audiobooks for the blind.*

CONTRIBUTOR ROLE

Every contributor should be listed alongside a contributor type or role. You may assign multiple roles to the same contributor if appropriate (e.g. for a book written and illustrated by one person).

Below are several of the most prominent contributor roles available and brief definitions. Please note that just because a particular role is not listed here does not mean it should not be used. All role types are valuable and every contributor you credit should be assigned a role.

- **By (author)**: A required role for any book that credits the primary author of a textual work. *Do not get this role confused with other similar "by" roles (such as "by (composer)" or "by (artist)") that serve a similar function but credit an entirely different person for an entirely different purpose. Likewise, don't confuse this role with the "text by" role, which should only be used when artwork or photography is a book's primary purpose, and the accompanying text serves a lesser purpose. (In this case, the author of this minor text would be credited using the "text by" role.)*

- **With**: This is used to credit any additional authors who would either not be considered primary or are credited within the book or in marketing materials as the "co-author."

- **Illustrated by**: This designates the artist who created any visual art illustrations within a textual work or created the art for a comic book or graphic novel. *It is important not to get this role confused with "by (artist)," which serves to credit an artist whose visual artwork is the primary topic of a particular book (such as a coffee table book about and filled with art by Andy Warhol, who would be credited as the "by (artist)").*

- **Cover design or artwork by**: The creator of either the cover art as a whole or any artwork used within the cover art.

- **Inker, colorist, or letterer**: Popular roles within comic books, used to describe either the inker, the person who inks lines of a previously drawn artwork; the colorist, the person who then follows the inker to color in the lines; or the letterer, the final person in the comic book drawing process who creates text balloons or other text elements. *The initial artist for the comic book (who did neither the inking nor the coloring) should be credited as "illustrated by."*

- **Read by**: Used specifically for readers of audiobooks. *The "narrator" role within ONIX is typically meant to credit narration in mediums outside of audiobooks. Depending on the system you are using to record metadata, sometimes either is fine.*

Do take into consideration the roles allowed by your internal systems and the external systems you deliver to. Depending on the standard you use, or if you're not using any sort of standard, there may be additional steps necessary to ensure that the roles you are storing within your internal systems are delivered and display properly in any external system.

> *Note on ONIX: See ONIX codelist 17 for all of the contributor roles supported within ONIX. It provides a great foundation for anyone looking to build a contributor type or role library to better credit their contributors.*

CONTRIBUTOR BIOGRAPHY

The contributor biography is recommended for all contributors, but it should be considered fundamental for authors and co-authors. These bios are frequently used on retail sites to provide additional information about the contributors.

The biography should be brief but packed with notable facts or achievements about the contributor, including:

- Important attributes, including relevant credentials and experience (particularly as pertinent to the specific work in question)

- Prior work and success, including other books, awards, and critical reception

- Related properties or associations, including businesses, institutions, media, or people the contributor is connected to

- Other activities and information that potential readers may find of interest, such as country or hometown, hobbies, and personal and professional pursuits

Biographies can include HTML markup, which we recommend to emphasize important points or works for the reader. (Note that HTML markup in text field-based metadata may include website addresses but should never contain an HTML hyperlink. Similarly, never include embedded HTML such as a contributor profile picture or a video introduction to the contributor. For further details regarding what is and isn't allowed in HTML for text field-based metadata, see page 52 for our section on HTML markup.)

The maximum character count for a contributor biography is 4,000 characters, but we advise keeping it well below this at about 50 to 150 words. While some contributors may warrant a larger biography, a short, concise bio always presents a much more digestible bite of information to the reader. Including time-sensitive information is also not recommended; a contributor biography should be written to remain relevant indefinitely.

Contributor Biography Example:

About the Author

Priscilla Royal, author of twelve books from Poisoned Pen Press in the Prioress Eleanor and Brother Thomas medieval mystery series, grew up in British Columbia and earned a BA in World Literature at San Francisco State University where she discovered the beauty of medieval literature. Before retiring from the Federal Government in 2000, she worked in a variety of jobs, all of which provided an excellent education in the complexity of human experience and motivation. She is a theater fan as well as a reader of history, mystery, and fiction of lesser violence. When not hiding in the thirteenth century, she lives in Northern California and is a member of California Writers Club, Mystery Writers of America, and Sisters in Crime.

Note on ONIX: If using ONIX, the contributor biography should be defined using the text type codelist (List 153).

CONTRIBUTOR LOCATION OR CONTRIBUTOR PLACE

Location-based metadata for a contributor (referred to as contributor location or contributor place) can convey many things:

- **Born in**: A contributor's location of birth.
- **Died in**: A contributor's location of death.

- **Formerly resided in**: Any past location(s) where the contributor does not currently live but has lived in the past.

- **Currently resides in**: The current-day location(s) where the contributor is living (or where they last lived before their death).

- **Educated in**: The location(s) the contributor received significant education (sometimes both geographic location and the name of the educational institution).

- **Worked in**: The location(s) where the contributor worked for a significant amount of time or had a specific, significant impact on an organization.

- **Flourished in**: This one may be tricky to pin down. A contributor's "flourished in" location(s) should be the place(s) where a contributor's most important life experiences or achievements occurred. For example, Mark Twain resided in Florida, Missouri, New York, Philadelphia, Ohio, Nevada, and Connecticut, but he wrote the majority of his classic novels while living in his custom-built home in Connecticut. Therefore, Connecticut would be considered his place of flourishing.

- **Citizen of**: The contributor's place of citizenship.

Proper and consistent formatting of location metadata is important to avoid data conflicts. A contributor located in the United States of America may have their "born in" location formatted by city, state, then country:

Hartford, Connecticut, United States of America

The proper formatting for each location may look slightly different depending on which country the contributor is located in, due to how different countries structure their localities. Keep your contributor country of origin in consideration when listing and formatting the proper contributor locations for all of the above metadata points.

For metadata such as "educated in" and "worked in," it is common to include a place of education, corporation, or company name. For example:

Yale University, New Haven, Connecticut, United States of America

> *Note on ONIX: If using ONIX, make sure that each contributor requiring multiple entries within the contributor place data point (such as a contributor who has lived in multiple past locations) also receives a separate data point and is properly defined using the contributor place relator codelist (List 151).*
>
> *The "citizen of" contributor place relator should always be accompanied with a country code matching the contributor's place of nationality.*

PRIOR WORKS & AFFILIATIONS

Listing a contributor's **prior works** may seem in conflict with listing past works within the contributor biography, but the key difference is that a contributor's prior works should be a comprehensive list of popular works the contributor has written or been involved with in the past. Works listed within the contributor biography should be considered their most popular; a wider listing of prior publications would bog down a biography and should be listed comprehensively under prior works instead.

When listing prior works, try to remember the following:

- Include any popular or important works that potential readers may be familiar with. These may be specific titles, series, characters, or collections.

- Separate listed works with a semicolon, comma, or line break.

This field does not replace the need to include important works by name in the contributor biography. It simply provides an independent data point to expand previously listed works or include others.

Note that "prior works" does not mean exclusively book titles. Any content or series-related information about the work that may be familiar or that you think readers might look for when searching for the book should be listed and considered under the prior work umbrella. (For example, you could mention that *The Magician's Nephew* is part of the Chronicles of Narnia series.)

Where prior works connect a contributor to other works, **affiliations** connect a contributor to corporations, organizations, or institutions they belong to. These may include:

- Businesses or nonprofits they have worked with

- Schools where they studied, taught, or conducted research (if studied, these affiliations should also be listed as "educated in" under contributor location)

- Clubs, groups, or professional associations

- Media or publications they have written for

As with prior works, affiliations should be separated with a semicolon, comma, or line break. Likewise, the affiliations metadata field does not overwrite any affiliations listed in the contributor biography but instead provides the opportunity for a more comprehensive list.

CONNECTING YOUR METADATA WITH IDS

When you take a step back and look at metadata as a whole, it's easy to get overwhelmed. Even when you zoom in and focus on the metadata for a single book, the number of data points is staggering if everything is properly accounted for. Once you start relating books to one another, associating contributors with other contributors, and factoring in different catalogs—well, things get crazy.

Identification codes (commonly referred to as IDs, or identity documents), both internal and external, help to make sure you know and keep track of all the intricate relationships between various pieces of metadata.

Common book industry identifiers include both product and contributor identifiers. All IDs allow you to connect the large amount of metadata associated with books and their contributors easily within any database system. When assigning IDs across your products, always ensure they are correct to avoid conflict within your own system. An ID is only good if it's consistently communicated throughout any catalog or digital merchant.

ISBN

The ISBN (or International Standard Book Number) has been the prominent standard product ID since its inception in the 1970s. It functions similarly to a UPC (Universal Product Code).

An ISBN is essential for any product, regardless of product form. It provides the underlying identification for a book within all internal catalogs and external services. Ensure that all products you are delivering, regardless of publishing or cataloging methods, are registered for a proper and complete ISBN code. A print ISBN is registered in the same manner as all other ISBN codes but should only be used alongside a physical printed product.

The modern ISBN is 13 digits long (in the past it was 10 digits) and structured like this:

978-3-16-148410-0

The 5 parts above, each separated by a dash each, represent the following:

- 978: GS1 prefix identifying the product; in an ISBN this is either 978 or 979

- 3: Registration group element; identifies the product's country or territory

- 16: Registrant element

- 148410: Publication element (identification within a publisher)

- 0: Check digit for error detection; helps to identify a legitimate ISBN

ISBNs are distributed per product on a country-to-country basis. Within the US, this service is provided by the Bowkor Identifier Services and Bowker, the U.S. ISBN Agency (isbn.org/). A full list of all ISBN distributors by country can be found on the International ISBN Agency's website (isbn-international.org/).

OTHER PRODUCT IDS

There are dozens of IDs throughout the book metadata world in addition to the ISBN. Publishers, retailers and distributors will often assign their own proprietary IDs at the product or product family level. These work family IDs help connect all formats and editions of the same title across product forms (such as an audiobook, ebook, and physical paperback) and across multiple publishers, providing a convenient linking element for a high-level view of your product.

Other custom internal IDs can be used to serve a similar function to be used within your own catalogs or distribution channels. ISBNs can be used as an internal ID, but we recommend also developing your own internal ID for large catalogs.

Note on ONIX: Within ONIX, product IDs are communicated through the product identifier type codelist (List 5).

ISNI

The ISNI (International Standard Name Identifier) functions similarly to the ISBN, serving as an international standard identification number that can link a single contributor across books as well as other forms of media. This cross-media capability is especially useful for catalogs with books, audio, and even video content. The ISNI is structured as such:

0000 001 2150 090X

Linking contributors across multiple forms of media allows for linkage across numerous databases. Using ISNI will let you effectively collect data for a contributor from other databases that use ISNI as well. One ISNI ID can link numerous recorded names to the same ID. The entry for William Shakespeare, for example, contains well over 100 name variations in multiple languages, as well as numerous "related names" (partners or corporations he was involved with) and "contributed to or performed" works.

All ISNI contributors are publicly available to view from the ISNI website.

ISNI standards are internationally managed by the UK company called the ISNI-IA. More information about ISNI can be found on the official website (isni.org/).

INDIGO & ISNI

Indigo is a major retailer that has invested in ISNI as an identifier within their online bookselling. Though their primary operations are in Canada, they have announced plans to test the US market as well. You might be more interested in investing in ISNI for your author metadata, particularly if the Canadian market is important to you.

LONG & SHORT DESCRIPTIONS

Your book description should be an accurate, compelling, and comprehensive guide to the inside of the book.

These best practices are designed to optimize your descriptive copy both for machines (e.g. Google and other search engines) and humans (potential readers considering the book) in general search and at retail.

LONG DESCRIPTION

A long description (often simply called the description) is exactly that: a detailed description of the work you're distributing.

Effective descriptive copy should meet established criteria and best practices for *structure*, *length*, and *content*, and it should provide rich, full information about the book.

HEADLINE *~200 characters* **Brief, bold "elevator pitch"**	• Start with a bold first line of approximately 25 words. • Include major topics, themes, and/or genres that potential readers might be searching for. • This is critical for SEO and discovery, and hooks buyers into reading more.
EXPOSITION *1+ paragraphs* **Clear, detailed description.**	• Give buyers the detail they need to make a purchasing decision. • Who or what is the book about? • Where and when is the story set? • What happens? • Use paragraph breaks, bold and italic fonts, and bullet points for emphasis.
CLOSE *Short paragraph* **Persuasive "why to buy"**	• Emphasize the value of the book, its intended audience, and your brand promise. • Who should buy this book? • What will they get out of it? • Why should they buy it now?

METADATA ESSENTIALS
Description

? THE BASICS

Detailed descriptive copy will help your book rank for relevant searches and convince readers to buy the book.

QUICK TIPS

✓ Include a detailed description of 200–4,000 characters.

✓ Use HTML markup and paragraph breaks to add structure and emphasis (see page 52).

✓ Use consumer keywords, topics, and phrases to optimize for search engines and potential buyers.

ESSENTIALS INDEX

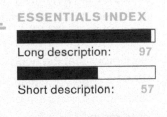

Long description: 97

Short description: 57

🛒 WHAT RETAILERS SAY

▪ **100%** display the **long description** to consumers.

▪ **67%** use the **short description.**

▪ **20%** use the description behind-the-scenes.

▪ Average accepted length: **1,200 words.**

Structure: Anatomy of a description

A well-constructed book description is critical for search engine optimization (SEO) and consumer conversion. **Proper description structure comes in three parts: the headline, a detailed exposition, and a strong close.**

HEADLINE

- Make it clear and punchy. Highlight the big things that matter about the book from a reader's perspective (genre, key topics and themes, major brands, awards). Get them to want to find out more or simply purchase based on what they've already seen.

- A headline should have a strong selling focus—less about plot and the specific details and more about why a busy reader should want this book. If someone didn't know the book existed, what might they be looking for that would bring them to this book?

- Remember that the headline will often be seen on retailer pages before consumers are prompted to "read more."

- Make the text **bold** and follow it with a paragraph break.

DETAILED EXPOSITION

- If a consumer clicks "read more," you want them to find rich details about the book.

- Convey the notable topics, themes, plot elements, and features of the book.

In Action: Headline

✗ Sam and Sally don't get along.

✔ A beautiful illustrated picture book about bullying, friendship, and learning to stand up for what's right.

In Action: Exposition

✗ In this book, the author presents some really lovely pictures that are good for all audiences. Throughout the 20 or so here, he talks about certain things that kids might be able to relate to, and people are sure to enjoy it. The best part of this book is the different colors the illustrator drew in—really vibrant and just a joy to look at.

✔ Are trees social beings? In this international bestseller, forester and author Peter Wohlleben convincingly makes the case that, yes, the forest is a social network. He draws on groundbreaking scientific discoveries to describe how trees are like human families: tree parents live together with their children, communicate with them, support them as they grow, share nutrients with those who are sick or struggling, and even warn each other of impending dangers. Wohlleben also shares his deep love of woods and forests, explaining the amazing processes of life, death, and regeneration he has observed in his woodland.

After learning about the complex life of trees, a walk in the woods will never be the same again.

- For fiction titles, describe the plot, settings, and key characters.

- For nonfiction, detail the subjects covered, as well as important people, places, and things.

- This is where you can "set the mood" and give readers an idea of the style and tone of the book.

- Use paragraph breaks and bulleted lists as appropriate to add structure and break up large blocks of text. (See page 52 for more on using HTML in your product description.)

STRONG CLOSE

- Emphasize why someone should buy the book. If a potential consumer has read this far, they are interested—now make the sale.

- Who is the book for? "Fans of....", "Great gift for..."

- Consider including awards, nominations, and/or a strong review quote. (If included here, do not exclude them for their respective specific metadata attributes.)

In Action: Close

✕ Check this book out when you can and definitely get it if you find it at a cheap price.

✔ Winner of the prestigious Newbery Medal in 1998, *Ella Enchanted* author Gail Carson Levine has conjured up another magical tale with *The Boy Magician*, a wondrous tale for children who seek out wonder and adventure.

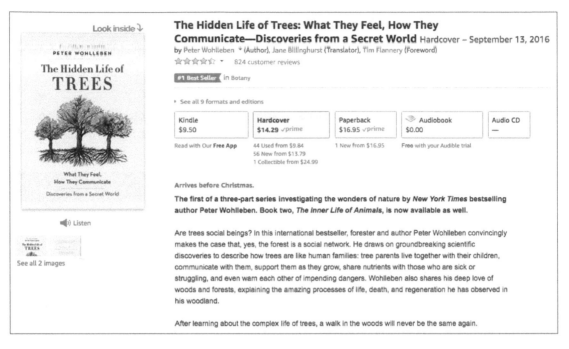

FIGURE 9. *Book description as seen on Amazon.com, captured December 2017.*

Content: What to include

While it is not essential to incorporate every element listed here, these are the major components that impact online discovery and consumer-purchasing decisions. We strongly recommend that you include them in the description when and as appropriate:

- Genres, topics, and themes
- Important and directly related people and brands
- Locations and time periods
- Special features and selling points specific to the edition or format
- Contributors' other titles, series, and awards
- Audience or age appropriateness
- Adjacent people, organizations, experience, media properties, and other important connections

- Bestseller history, critical reception, and awards (these can be retroactively added to a description following the book's initial sales cycle)

KEYWORDS

Use consumer keywords, topics, and phrases to align your description with the ways in which potential buyers talk about and look for books. Speak their language!

See page 70 for more on using keywords to improve discovery.

HTML

HTML markup is accepted by most retailers in the description, and you should use it to include formatted and structured content:

- Use paragraph breaks to break up large blocks of text, making the description easier for search engines and human beings to parse.

- Bold and italic text provides emphasis and draws attention to important points.

- Bullet points are useful (for nonfiction descriptions in particular) to highlight key aspects of the book.

See page 52 for more detail on using HTML to create easy-to-read and thorough descriptions.

LENGTH

We recommend an overall copy length of 200–750 words, though some books will lend themselves more readily to longer descriptions than others. Typically, the more information you can provide, the better.

Within ONIX, the description has no real text limit, but most distribution platforms will place a character limit on it to prevent extremes. **We recommend a maximum of 4,000 characters and a minimum of 200 characters.**

SHORT DESCRIPTION

The short description can be thought of almost as an expanded headline (detailed on page 36). The short description should vividly and precisely describe what a consumer would want to know about the book in as few characters as possible, while also conveying what sets it apart from other novels that may share similarities.

Often distributors will display the short description and cover art or brief metadata about your book alongside various other products, so it's important that your book's cover art and short description deliver a one-two punch that compels consumers to dive in and learn more.

The ONIX character limit for a short description is 350 characters, **but we recommend something even more concise, around 150 to 200 characters.**

While the short description is very similar to the headline described above, never just repeat your headline. The short description and long description are rarely displayed side-by-side and should work in tandem to complement each other and provide a rich and vivid narrative. The short description should house what you believe buyers will find most important, prompting them to take the next step to the long description, where further attractive details await in the headline and beyond.

1 Contains certain content from a listing at https://www.amazon.com/Lion-Witch-Wardrobe-ChroniclesNarnia/dp/0064404994/

BOOK CATEGORIES & SUBJECT CODES

Subject codes help signal to potential buyers, retailers and search engines what your book is about—the primary genre(s), topic(s), and theme(s) that matter.

Perhaps one of the most controversial sources of contention within book metadata are BISAC codes and other similar subject code standards. Very few pieces of metadata, when inputted incorrectly or sloppily, cause a larger mess across both cataloging and marketing. It would be impossible to call this a list of metadata essentials without breaking down important types of subject codes and outlining several spots where things tend to go awry.

BISAC

BISAC (Book Industry Standards and Communications) subject codes are the most common subject identifiers for books across numerous standards. There are hundreds of new BISAC codes added annually, and it's important to keep up with the complete list of BISAC codes (bisg.org/page/BISACEdition) when considering specific headings for new releases. **With so many subjects to choose from, there are almost guaranteed to be several specific codes that match any one individual product. When choosing those subject codes, you need to be as specific as possible.**

Below are several tips for choosing a good BISAC code:

- One BISAC code is required, but three is considered best practice to help ensure the broadcast reach for the book.
- If possible, select from multiple top-level BISAC subject headings to broaden discovery.

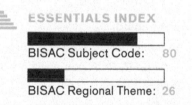

- Avoid *General* codes whenever possible. (This is especially true for *FIC000000 FICTION / General.*)
- BISAC codes should be consistent across different formats of the same work.
- Use the subject code *NON000000 NON-CLASSIFIABLE* for any book that does not contain any content (such as a blank book). Never use this code outside of rare no-content-book situations.

UNDERSTANDING BISAC CODES

BISAC subject codes are comprised of three primary parts:

Subject Heading

High-level genres and topics such as *BIOGRAPHY & AUTOBIOGRAPHY*, *RELIGION*, and *FICTION* that cover a wide umbrella of more specific topics, serving essentially as a category for more particular subjects. One book can—and should, if possible—have more than one subject heading.

- *HISTORY*
- *GARDENING*
- *FICTION*

Subheading

The numerous subjects contained within each subject heading. For example, under the heading *FICTION* you may find subheadings such as *African American*, *Romance*, and *Science Fiction.*

Each subject heading will commonly have an individual *General* subheading that should be avoided. More detailed and refined subheadings are recommended whenever possible. The more specific, the better.

- *BUSINESS & ECONOMICS / Bookkeeping*
- *HISTORY / Middle East / Arabian Peninsula*
- *FICTION / Mystery & Detective / Cozy / Cats & Dogs*

Code

The nine-character alphanumeric reference code assigned to each specific subheading.

- *JUV048000   JUVENILE FICTION / Clothing & Dress*
- *TEC009100   TECHNOLOGY & ENGINEERING / Civil / Bridges*
- *FIC028030   FICTION / Science Fiction / Space Opera*

STAY UP TO DATE

Most distribution or cataloging software will contain up-to-date BISAC codes for use when filling out the metadata for your book. For those that use their own distribution or cataloging (via ONIX or otherwise), ensure that your BISAC code library is up to date. BISAC subject codes are updated annually, and these updates include adding various new subjects as well as changing existing ones, either by removing and replacing with new subjects or by moving them under different subject headings. Stay conscious of these updates and be vigilant in confirming that your BISAC library is up to date.

ORDER MATTERS

Second only to the accuracy of your BISAC subject codes is the order in which you place them. While it may seem like a trivial thing to place more precise subjects first, this decision has numerous practical benefits within cataloging systems and search engine optimization. **The first subject code should be the best, most accurate, and most specific code possible.**

See the order below for a good example of this:

1. *FICTION / Christian / Futuristic*
2. *FICTION / Science Fiction / General*
3. *RELIGION / Philosophy*

Utilizing the three subject codes in that order above could accurately describe a sci-fi novel about a future Christian society that contains numerous themes related to a philosophical Christian concept. The most specific code, *FICTION / Christian / Futuristic*, is listed first, followed by a less specific *FICTION / Science Fiction / General*, followed lastly by a broad *RELIGION / Philosophy*.

BISAC CODES AND CHILDREN'S BOOKS

For any book aimed at children or young adults, you must include a relevant subject code in at least one of the three BISAC codes. (See page 48 for more on age and audience data.) Never use *JUVENILE* and *YOUNG ADULT* subject codes outside of their allowed age ranges.

- Age range for children from 0 to 11 (Preschool through grade 6)
  Requires at least one subject code under either the *JUVENILE FICTION* (JUV) or *JUVENILE NONFICTION* (JNF) subject headings.

- Age range for young readers and teens ages 12 to 18 (Grades 7 through 12)
  Requires at least one subject code under either the *YOUNG ADULT FICTION* (YAF) or *YOUNG ADULT NONFICTION* (YAN) subject headings.

These requirements allow for concise cataloging for publishers, librarians, and others. This also guarantees that any juvenile or young adult books distributed will be placed in their proper sections across both physical and digital marketplaces.

BISAC REGIONAL THEMES VS COUNTRY OF ORIGIN

BISAC regional themes are used in conjunction with BISAC codes to provide information on the primary geographic location of the book. It's important not to confuse this location with the country of origin. For any one product, the country of origin is the single country where a product was originally developed and/or published. The regional subject code, on the other hand, relates to the actual content of the book. For example, *Outlander* would contain the following:

Regional Theme: Scotland
- The book mostly takes place in Scotland in the 18th century.

Country of Origin: United States
- The book is written by American Diana Gabaldon and published in the United States on June 1, 1991.

The country of origin for a product should be defined using its proper country code and should remain constant through the entire product's lifetime. Conversely, the regional theme should be defined using the layered codes developed to work alongside BISAC codes. You can view a complete list of those codes on the BISAC Regional Themes List section (bisg.org/page/BISACRegionalTheme) of the BISG website.

Note on ONIX: If using ONIX, BISAC codes and regional themes codes can be communicated and defined via the main subject scheme identifier codelist (List 26) and subject scheme identifier codelist (List 27).

THEMA FOR INTERNATIONAL TRADE

Thema, when used properly, provides an extremely precise subject code that can be easily used across numerous countries. We recommend giving your book both BISAC and Thema subjects to cover all possible ground.

> *Note on BIC: BIC (Book Industry Communication) subject categories codes were discontinued in late 2017 in favor of further development and support Thema subject categories. Thema is a natural evolution of BIC subject categories, both in structure and use. Older titles categorized using BIC codes should be retrofitted with Thema as well.*

Compared to BISAC, a traditionally North American-based standard, Thema was developed for international use. Thema codes are structurally more complex than BISAC codes and require a deeper knowledge to assure you are assigning the proper code to your book.

Thema schemes are broken up into two sections:
- Subject categories
- Qualifiers (including national extensions)

THEMA SUBJECT CATEGORIES

Subject categories are the part of Thema that most resembles BISAC subject codes, with around 2,500 subcategories spread out over 20 top-level

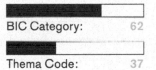

categories. A common subject category may look like this, where the starting "A" represents the top-level category (*The Arts*) and the code as a whole, "AGA," represents the specific subcategory within it (*History of art*):

      AGA   History of art

This hierarchy allows you to assign a single Thema subject category to a book that potentially covers multiple sections. You don't need to include higher-level subject or qualifier codes if you have already selected a more specific code for a given category or subcategory (e.g. *JPSD Society & Social Sciences / Politics & government / International relations / Diplomacy* is understood to be about society and social sciences (*J*), international relations (*JP*), and politics and government (*JPS*).

THEMA QUALIFIERS

Qualifiers are unique to Thema schemes, allowing you to assign as many or as few additional details to a subject category as needed. Each qualifier falls into one of six sections:

- Place: Locations and regions important to the work (similar to BISAC regional themes)
        E.g. *1HFGU   Uganda*

- Language: Languages or dialects the book is about (not what the book is written in)
        E.g. *2ACSC   Icelandic*

- Time period: Eras, centuries and important historical events
        E.g. *3MD   16th century, c 1500 to c 1599*

- Educational purpose: School or grade level, language learning or training materials
        E.g. *4GH   For International GCSE (IGCSE)*

- Interest age and special interest: Reading age or level (for children's books); holidays, special events, and seasonal interests; intended use by particular groups or cultures (e.g. women and girls, ethnic or religious groups, LGBT community)
        E.g. *5AG   Interest age: From c 6 years*

- Style: Artistic or creative styles either covered by the work (e.g. Art Deco, pop art, tango) or exemplified by the work (e.g. postmodernism, elegy, avant garde)
        E.g. *6BA   Baroque*

We recommend using a maximum of 5 subject codes and 5 qualifier codes (for each subject code), though either fewer or more are acceptable. Always use whatever amount you feel is appropriate and most specifically describes your book.

NATIONAL EXTENSIONS

National extensions are what solidify Thema as an international standard, allowing you to assign country-specific extensions to qualifiers that are easily understood in any language. Below are several examples of these extensions:

- 1DNS-SE-BH   Västergötland, Sweden
  Derived from 1DNS   Sweden

- 3MPBGJ-ES-B   Spain: Civil war (1936-1939)
  Derived from 3MPBGJ   c 1930 to c 1939

- 4Z-UK-SD   Scottish Curriculum National 5
  Derived from 4Z   For specific national curricula

- 5HC-US-A   US Independence Day
  Derived from 5HC   Holidays and celebrations

If we dissect the second example above, we can better understand what makes these national extensions tick (and the power they offer in providing ultra-specific subject information):

- 3MPBGJ: Qualifier for subjects in the time period c 1930 to c 1939

- ES: National extension for Spain

- B: For books referring to the Spanish Civil War

We highly recommend checking out the EDItEUR website's resources (editeur.org/files/Thema/20160601%20Thema%20v1.2%20Basic%20instructions.pdf) **on Thema for further instructions and examples to ensure proper use.**

AUDIENCE INFORMATION

There are three primary attributes for relaying audience information to retailers and other channel partners:

- Audience code
- Audience range or age range
- Complexity & reading levels

Audience code is required for all books. Additional age range and complexity information are critical for children's, young adult, and teen books and is especially useful for librarians.

AUDIENCE CODE

The audience code is used to properly assign a broad audience to a product. **Always strive to use the most correct and most specific audience code that describes the primary audience for your book.**

Trade/consumer audiences:

- General/trade: for general adult consumer audiences
- Children/juvenile: for juvenile or general children's audiences, but not for any specific educational purpose
- Young adult: for young adult or teen audiences, but not for any specific educational purpose

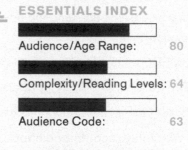

Specialty audiences:

- Primary, secondary/elementary, and high school
- College/higher education
- Professional and scholarly

- ELT/ESL
- Adult education
- Second-language teaching

As stated in the BISAC section, only use the *JUVENILE-* and *YOUNG ADULT*-related BISAC subject headings if the audience code matches. Any conflict between audience codes and BISAC subject headings can cause delay or disruption in distribution.

In contrast to BISAC codes, the *General* audience code is more accepted if another audience is not appropriate.

> *Note on ONIX: Audience codes are outlined within the ONIX audience code codelist (List 28). If using ONIX, use the audience code type (List 29) to clarify that you are using the ONIX audience codes. This codelist should also be used to identify any other audience codes outside of the ONIX standard (such as a proprietary code, MPAA ratings, or Nielsen Books audience codes).*

AUDIENCE RANGE

The audience range allows you to get much more granular, providing specific age or grade ranges for a book. This is mandatory for all juvenile and young adult audiences.

Tips for audience range:

- For what age group is the book intended? Specify both **age** and **grade level** ranges when possible.

- Audience range is also recommended for mature graphic novels and other works that may be confused as children's titles.

- **The range should be as realistic and as specific as possible.** Your potential buyers are using this guidance to understand the primary intended audience for the book.

- Keep ranges narrow, particularly for young children (just two years or grade levels).

- For teen audiences, ranges may be broader (up to four years or grade levels).

- You may also specify a separate **reading age** (specified in List 30 in ONIX) for high-low titles, where the reading level may be different from the maturity level of the content. (This should be used carefully in conjunction with appropriate complexity information. If you do not have a professional assessment of the reading age for a book, do not use this field.)

Audience Range Example:

    Qualifier: 11 - US school grade range

    From: P - Preschool

    To: 3 - Third Grade

> *Note on ONIX: Within ONIX, the audience range qualifier (List 30) and audience range precision (List 31) allow you to specify a range within various country standards. Take care to be as specific as possible when outlining an audience range. Listing an improper audience range, especially if it conflicts with the audience code or other age-related pieces of metadata, will lead to distribution delays and other data inconsistencies.*

COMPLEXITY & READING LEVEL

Identifying the complexity and reading level of your book may seem redundant when also providing an audience code and audience range. However, reading levels may be much more useful for certain consumers, buyers, and readers (especially in education) who are looking for a more specific representation of a book's complexity in relation to children's reading levels.

You may specify complexity under several different reading level standards, including Lexile, Fountas and Pinnell, ATOS, Flesch-Kincaid, and others. We recommend always using Lexile codes to define readability for any juvenile titles with appeal to the educational market, especially for releases aligned with Common Core standards. An example of a Lexile measure code is:

    Lexile Measure: 570L

See Chapter 4, page 114 for more on complexity ratings, reading programs, and how libraries use this data to understand readability and appropriateness for young readers.

ONIX Example:

```
<Complexity>
      <ComplexitySchemeIdentifier>06</ComplexitySchemeIdentifier>
            <ComplexityCode>570L</ComplexityCode>
</Complexity>
```

Note on ONIX: ONIX provides a connection to many reading level standards within the complexity scheme identifier codelist (List 32).

HTML FOR BOOK METADATA

Using simple HTML (Hypertext Markup Language) **leads to better, easier-to-read metadata that improves search engine optimization and consumer conversion.**

We recommend utilizing HTML for the following metadata elements:

- Description
- Contributor biography
- Table of contents
- Index

Note that any HTML used within these fields will count towards the overall character count.

PARAGRAPHS AND LINE BREAKS

Long, text-based metadata attributes should include paragraphs to break up the text. This is especially important in your book descriptive copy.

- Paragraph tags (<p>Example text.</p>) are the preferred method for creating paragraph breaks.

- Paragraphs should be enclosed with start (<p>) and end (</p>) paragraph tags.

- Alternately, you can use two consecutive line break tags (e.g.

) to create visual space between two paragraphs.

- Line break variations include: <br>, <br/>, <br />, or </br>.

- Using consecutive line breaks can sometimes lead to larger-than-intended spaces between paragraphs.

HTML Input	Result
`<p>Example text! Example text.</p>` `<p>Example text.</p>`	Example text! Example text. Example text.
`Example text! Example` `text.  Example text.`	Example text! Example text. Example text.

BASIC TEXT FORMATTING

Use simple HTML formatting to produce more useful and readable metadata text. The most commonly used and supported text formatting include:

- `<b>` or `<strong>` for **bold** text
- `<em>` or `<i>` for *italicized* text
- `<u>` for <u>underlined</u> text

Formatted text should be properly enclosed with a beginning and ending tag, and tags should be in lowercase.

HTML Input	Result
`<b>Example text!</b>` or `<strong>Example text!</strong>`	**Example text!**
`<i>Example text!</i>` or `<em>Example text!</em>`	*Example text!*
`<u>Example text!</u>`	<u>Example text!</u>

LISTS

Use bulleted and numbered lists to highlight key features of your book in the product description or to properly structure your table of contents.

- Use <ul> to identify bulleted (unordered) lists and <ol> for numbered (ordered) lists.

- Once you have specified the type of list, use <li> to identify individual items in the list.

- Be sure to close each list item (</li>) and then close the list itself (</ul> or </ol>).

    List tags must be appropriately nested and properly closed.

HTML Input	Result
```<ul> <li>Bullet list item one</li> <li>List item two</li> <li>Another list item</li> </ul>```	• Bullet list item one • List item two • Another list item
```<ol> <li>Numbered list item one</li> <li>List item two</li> <li>Another list item</li> </ol>```	1. Numbered list item one 2. List item two 3. Another list item

INSIDER TIP: HTML EDITORS

There are lots of free HTML editors available online to show you a side-by-side view of your HTML tags and what your data will look like online. Try the W3Schools HTML editor (w3schools.com/html/tryit.asp?filename=tryhtml_basic) or do a quick search for "free html editor" to find a version that works for you.

Note on ONIX: ONIX allows for HTML and other markup, but not all data senders or recipients handle this the same way. Check with your metadata management team or data partner for any restrictions on the use of HTML and special characters in your product data. XHTML is strongly recommended over HTML for both ONIX 2.1 and 3.0 (textformat="05") to ensure validation and improved display across data recipients. Note that with XHTML, all tags must be properly closed and must be in lowercase.

RELATED PRODUCTS

Related product information is used by many booksellers and libraries. You can provide information about other formats and editions of the work as well as comparable title data to inform booksellers of comps for sales expectations.

OTHER FORMATS AND EDITIONS

Use related products to specify alternate formats and editions of your book. This data informs and improves online search functionality and helps retailers and libraries understand how different products are connected to one another, including:

- Other formats of the work (e.g. corresponding print, ebook, audio, or large print editions)

- Prior editions of the work (especially for titles that have been updated, where the new edition replaces the previous)

- A print-on-demand replacement for an out-of-print title

- Titles included in a compilation or bundle

- Related ancillary or supplementary products

- Special editions

- Alternate language editions

- Other works by the same author or in the same series

 METADATA ESSENTIALS
Related Products

THE BASICS
Related products help ensure your book is appropriately connected to other formats and editions as well as to comp titles.

QUICK TIPS
✓ Include related product identifiers (ISBNs) for different formats of the book.
✓ Make sure to link corresponding print, ebook, and audio editions of the same work.
✓ Comparable titles are useful in catalog platforms like Edelweiss to assist bookstores and libraries in making purchasing decisions.

ESSENTIALS INDEX

Related Products: 70

WHAT RETAILERS SAY
- 43% use related products either onsite for consumers or for internal purposes.

Note on ONIX: See ONIX codelist 51 for all available product relation codes. The most commonly used related format and edition types are:

Code	Definition	Relationship
13	Epublication based on (print product)	Is an e-publication based on specified print work
27	Electronic version available	Has a related e-publication (*for print publications*)
06	Alternative version available	Has an alternative version (e.g. audio)

The 13 and 27 codes are reciprocals of one another for related print and ebook formats.

Here is an example composite for the *Dream Hoarders* hardcover, giving a related ebook format:

```
<RelatedProduct>
    <RelationCode>27</RelationCode>              27 is the "ebook also available" code
    <ProductIdentifier>
        <ProductIDType>15</ProductIDType>        15 means 13-digit ISBN
        <IDValue>9780815729136</IDValue>         This is the ebook ISBN
    </ProductIdentifier>
</RelatedProduct>
```

Here is an example of the reciprocal composite for the ebook format, indicating a related hardcover book:

```
<RelatedProduct>
    <RelationCode>13</RelationCode>              13 is the "print also available" code
    <ProductIdentifier>
        <ProductIDType>15</ProductIDType>        15 means 13-digit ISBN
        <IDValue>9780815729129</IDValue>         This is the hardcover ISBN
    </ProductIdentifier>
</RelatedProduct>
```

COMPARABLE AND SIMILAR TITLES

Related product information also allows you to specify similar and comparable titles. These are used primarily by the catalog platforms like Edelweiss (edelweiss.plus), but distributors in both the physical and digital space may also set up venues for your book to be visible alongside related books that share themes or writing styles.

Above the Treeline highly recommends including 1 to 6 comparable titles on Edelweiss to provide retail/wholesale buyers, librarians, and media types with additional information when making purchasing decisions.

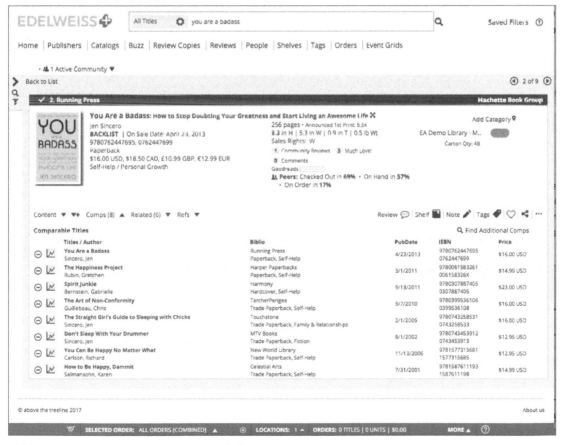

FIGURE 10. *Comparable titles as shown in Edelweiss Plus.*

Note on ONIX: Comparable titles are specified within the related products composite. See ONIX codelist 51 for all available product relation codes.

Code	Definition	Relationship
36	Sales expectations	Has comparable sales estimate and expectations (in terms of both number of copies sold and audience/consumer profile)
03	Replaces	<Product> replaces, or is new edition of, <RelatedProduct>
23	Similar Product	Has a suggested similar work (e.g. people who like <RelatedProduct> will also like this <Product>)

TERRITORIAL RIGHTS

Territory data is important to ensure the broad and accurate distribution of your book. Your sales rights data should be as detailed as necessary to clarify where your book may (or may not) be sold.

- Specify where your book should be available for sale (and whether you hold either exclusive or nonexclusive rights in those territories).

- Specify where your book should not be available for sale.

- Avoid listing long strings of territories, as they are messy, often difficult to understand, and prone to errors.

- Use WORLD and ROW (rest of world) designations as appropriate to be concise.

   Be careful when defining the territorial rights for your book's distribution, or you may accidentally bar it from release in approved territories.

METADATA ESSENTIALS
Territorial Rights

? THE BASICS
Accurate information on sales rights and restrictions is critical to ensure your book is made available for sale in the proper territories (and not sold where you do not have rights).

QUICK TIPS
✓ Keep your rights statements simple and specific.
✓ Use proper country or region codes to include and exclude given territories.
✓ Use WORLD and ROW (rest of world) designations to help avoid listing long strings of territories.

ESSENTIALS INDEX

Territory Rights: 69

 WHAT RETAILERS SAY
▪ Most retailers who use territory restrictions use it to filter unsupported titles from the catalog.

Note on ONIX: See ONIX codelist 46 for all available sales rights types. You may use multiple territorial rights statements, but only include each sales rights type once.

Use the proper country and region codes to identify any territories where you do or do not want the book distributed.

- *Specify regions as outlined in ONIX codelist 49.*

- *Specify countries as outlined in ONIX codelist 91.*

- *You may include multiple regions or country codes as needed, each separated by a space.*

- *"ROW" / "Rest of world" territory code is not supported in ONIX 3.0. Instead you should use the <ROWSalesRightsType> element to clarify sales rights for all territories not otherwise specified.*

- *Generally, depending on the system you are using, any country that is not specified within territorial restrictions will automatically be considered "approved."*

<u>ONIX Example:</u>
For sale with exclusive world rights, excluding Great Britain, Australia, and New Zealand.

```
<SalesRights>
        <SalesRightsType>01</SalesRightsType>
        <Territory>
        <RegionsIncluded>WORLD</RegionsIncluded>
        <CountriesExcluded>GB AU NZ</CountriesExcluded>
        </Territory>
</SalesRights>

<ROWSalesRightsType>06</ ROWSalesRightsType>
```

PRODUCT FORM AND OTHER HIGH-LEVEL PRODUCT DETAILS

The metadata described in this section serves as the foundation of your book and allows for base-level proper visibility across all merchants. This core product form information allows you to specify the type or format of the book, as well as any distinguishing features that set it apart from other related formats.

PRODUCT FORM

What is the primary format of your product?
This is the most basic level of metadata and is generally a minimum requirement by book distributors. Product form data is necessary for both physical and digital product types.

Product forms for physical products include things like:

- Hardback
- Paperback
- Pamphlet
- Sheet music

Other less common physical product forms include game cartridges, filmstrips, and stickers.

Product forms for digital products include things like:

- Digital online (streamed content)
- Digital download (download-only content)
- Digital product license

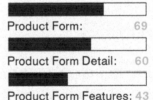

Some primarily physical product forms can also be applied to digital products if they are valid and appropriate.

> Note on ONIX: See ONIX codelist 150 for the complete list of product form types. For products made up of multiples forms or pieces (e.g. a multi-disk audio CD set or a board book and plush toy set), use product form to specify the primary format and the <NumberOfPieces> and/or <ContainedItem> composites to specify additional parts.

PRODUCT FORM DETAIL

If we dive down another level, we arrive at product form detail. This includes things such as audio file formats and types of paperbacks. It is highly recommended to include a product form detail when available. **The more detail you provide, the more channel partners will be able to understand and organize your product both universally within their store and relationally alongside other similar products.** This helps ensure that people who are browsing books similar to yours will also get their eyes on your product.

Common physical product form details include:

- Coloring/join-the-dot book
- Miniature book
- Picture book
- Trade paperback
- Material attributes of the product (such as leather, real, and flexible plastic/vinyl cover)

Product form details for physical products are often territory-related. For example, the *Kartonnage* and *Storpocket* details are only used for Swedish products. Ensure that you do not use territorial-based details that are not supported in your desired distribution territories.

Common digital product form details include:

- MP3 format
- WAV format
- Audible (proprietary format for Audible.com)
- Readalong audio
- Playalong audio

Digital products may have more than one product form detail, such as *MP3 format* and *Readalong audio* detailing a children's educational audiobook stored as a MP3 file.

Note on ONIX: See ONIX codelist 175 for the complete list of product form detail types. You may specify multiple product form detail codes if appropriate.

PRODUCT FORM FEATURE

Product form features are even more detailed descriptions of special features and aspects of a product. These are important for certain specialty publishers and may be valuable for general publishers depending on the book.

Common product form features include:

- Text font used for body text (important for large print works and Bibles)
- Accessibility of e-publications
- E-publication format and version information

- Certifications (FSC, PEFC)
- Hazard warnings
- Color of cover or page edge
- Paper produced by green technology

Product form features reach across both physical and digital products and are some of the most minute pieces of metadata you can supply.

Note on ONIX: See ONIX codelist 79 for the complete list of product form features and any further instructions or detail needed.

MEASUREMENTS

Consumers, retailers, and other channel partners rely on your metadata to accurately describe your product. For physical products, this includes accurate size and weight measurements to aid in purchasing, inventory management, and merchandising decisions.

Measurements you may specify:

- Height or length down the spine of the book
- Width across the top edge of the cover, perpendicular to the spine
- Depth or thickness across the spine
- Weight of a single product unit

   For each, you should also specify the unit of measurement—whether you are measuring in grams, inches, centimeters, etc. If using inches, specify down to the nearest eight of an inch, and for ounces, specify down the nearest quarter of an ounce.

> Note on ONIX: See the relevant ONIX codelist for detail on supported measure types (List 48) and measure units (List 50).

Example Measure: Height

```
<Measure>
        <MeasureType>01</MeasureType>
        <Measurement>150</Measurement>
        <MeasureUnitCode>mm</MeasureUnitCode>
</Measure>
```

Example Measure: Unit Weight

```
<Measure>
        <MeasureType>08</MeasureType>
        <Measurement>3</Measurement>
        <MeasureUnitCode>lb</MeasureUnitCode>
</Measure>
```

DATE & DIGITAL PRE-ORDERS

ENABLING PRE-ORDERS

Most retailers require a minimum of product data, including key dates, to enable pre-order sales. This information should be sent to retail channel partners as early as possible.

Data required for digital pre-orders

Pub Date	85.7%
Title	85.7%
Price	85.7%
On Sale Date	80.9%
Cover Image	76%
File Received Date	28.5%

Additional descriptive product metadata and marketing copy, like your description, BISAC subject codes, and more, will also help improve your chances for pre-order sales.

You must then send the ebook file prior to the stated on sale date to avoid lost sales and delays in delivery.

How retailers manage pre-orders if the ebook file is not delivered on time

Remove from sale	44.4%
Push pub date out	33%
Send alert to publisher/distributor to change date	22%

? THE BASICS

Include key timeline data to enable digital pre-orders and communicate when a book should be delivered to buyers.

QUICK TIPS

✓ Send publishing date and on sale date to enable online pre-order sales.
✓ These will typically be the same date.
✓ Make sure retailers have the ebook file prior to the on sale date to avoid delays in distribution and delivery.

ESSENTIALS INDEX

Date: 64

🛒 WHAT RETAILERS SAY

▪ **50%** of retailers accept digital pre-orders if key product data is supplied.
▪ **44%** of retailers will remove a product from sale if the ebook file is not delivered prior to the on sale date.

ABOUT DATES

We recommended including the following date alongside all your products to properly track and reference any necessary dates when needed:

- Publishing date
- On sale date
- File received date

A product's **publishing date** and **on sale date** are often the same. A book's publishing date will only differ from its on sale date when it's a work that has been previously published. Keeping track of both dates is important, however, in case a new edition of a previously published book is released down the road.

The **file received date** is important for a publisher to know, and it generally will remain an internal piece of metadata. This date indicates when you have received a book from an author and, in combination with the publishing date and on sale date, can provide a comprehensive timeline of the book's life within your catalogue.

> *Note on ONIX: All date formats should be properly defined within ONIX (where applicable) using the date format codelist (List 55). The most common format is YYYYMMDD, and whatever format you choose should be consistent across all dates recorded within your catalog metadata.*

Example to Enable Pre-orders:

```
<SupplyDetail>
      <OnSaleDate>YYYYMMDD</OnSaleDate>
</SupplyDetail>
```

ILLUSTRATION & OTHER IMAGE DETAILS

The primary reason for detailing exactly what types of images and illustrations your book contains is the same as for indicating that there is a glossary: informing your consumer. The more metadata surrounding your book, the more a consumer can learn from a simple product page, and the more likely it is that a sale will be made.

Including these details also serves for cataloging products and helping to know the difference between different editions of a book (for instance, where one edition may have color illustrations and the other black-and-white).

There is a large variety of images and illustrations you should specify, including illustrations, line drawings, tables, maps, diagrams, figures, and charts. While we highly recommend always identifying any image or illustration types within a product, the most essential to identify are:

- Illustrations
- Halftones (used for photographs)
- Line drawings
- Tables
- Maps
- Plates

Most illustration types include an option to specify either black and white or color. There is also an "unspecified" color option, which you should avoid using at all costs.

Note that this should never be used for identifying front and back cover art.

For both illustrations and maps, a matching contributor and contributor role of either "illustrated by" or "maps by" is necessary. If the name of the illustrator or mapper (or map contributor) is not available, check back in our contributor section on the steps you can take to credit an anonymous contributor.

Note on ONIX: See ONIX codelist 25 for a complete list of illustration, image, and other content types that may be specified. Credit inset maps apart from other more standard maps (e.g. "Larger-scale inset maps of places or features of interest included in a map product").

KEYWORDS

Keywords improve product discovery and categorization by aligning your book with how likely consumers may look for it or books like it. This requires a delicate balance of high-level keywords that cast a broad net and more specific keywords that narrowly describe the smaller details.

Our tips for producing better keywords are:

- Use at least 7 keyword phrases, semicolon separated with no space after the semicolon.

- Author, book title, contributor names, or other pieces of specific metadata credited elsewhere should not be used as keywords.

- Do not duplicate keywords used in the book description or other descriptive metadata attributes.

- Do not put quotation marks around any keywords.

- Do not include common misspellings or deviations of one keyword.

- Different "versions" are acceptable (e.g. MD and doctor; iPad and iPad Pro), as are synonyms.

When developing your keywords, always think like a reader. Consider how readers and potential buyers talk about the book (or similar books), what topics they care about, and the search phrases they might use to find the book.

METADATA ESSENTIALS
Keywords

? THE BASICS
Use keywords to improve online retail categorization and search engine optimization.

QUICK TIPS
- ✓ Word to the wise: while some retailers may or may not use keywords, Amazon definitely does.
- ✓ Include at least 7 keywords, topics, and phrases.
- ✓ Put the most relevant, important, and "big" ones first.
- ✓ Keyword phrases should be likely consumer search terms that highlight the breadth and depth of potential interest in the book.
- ✓ Use keyword phrases that complement (but don't replicate) the book descriptive copy.

ESSENTIALS INDEX

Keywords: 34

🛒 WHAT RETAILERS SAY
- About **35%** of retailers use keyword data behind the scenes for internal purposes.
- **17%** display them onsite for customers.

The most useful keywords fall under one of the following:

- Specific retailer product categories (that do not have an equivalent BISAC code)
- Important topics and themes (e.g. Mediterranean diet)
- Important locations or time periods from the book (e.g., Victorian era; American Southwest)
- Story tone, writing style, and/or genre (e.g. psychological thriller)
- Character types and roles (e.g. immigrant kids)
- Format or audience notes (e.g. coloring books)

Keywords should be used in the way that most effectively helps consumers find books. **Overall, more specific keywords are better.**

Example 1:

Overloaded keyword list to describe *The Hobbit, or There and Back Again*:

Fantasy; mystery; heroes; champions; people; castles; dragons; wizards; evil; gold; adventure; men; women; children; giants; trolls; bad guys; good guys; children's book; all ages; Tolkien; J.R.R. Tolkien; short book

This list will ultimately be less successful than a more precise list that targets what your suspected audience will be searching for and allows for proper categorization:

Medieval fantasy; Middle-Earth; hobbits; dwarves; wizards; epic quest; children's fantasy novel

Example 2:

Keywords for *Talking Back, Talking Black: Truths About America's Lingua Franca*:

Black English; American dialects; black lives matter; TED talk speaker

FICTION KEYWORD BRAINSTORMING SHEET

Use the wheel below to brainstorm useful and relevant keyword selections for your fiction titles. Increase discoverability by adding at least 7 keywords to your title's metadata.

NONFICTION KEYWORD BRAINSTORMING SHEET

Use the wheel below to brainstorm useful and relevant keyword selections for your nonfiction titles. Increase discoverability by adding at least 7 keywords to your title's metadata.

CHAPTER 3: Major Bookseller Profiles

Many of our insights in this book are based on a detailed survey of 60 booksellers and book-discovery sites worldwide and revealed key facts about their reliance on metadata for ordering, stocking, and merchandising books. In Chapter 3, we'll drill into the responses we gathered and take a look at how individual data elements are used by major retailers, including Amazon, Barnes & Noble, Walmart, Books-a-Million, and others. We'll discuss important trends in the demand for metadata, and you'll find tips for tailoring your information to meet the needs of specific sellers.

OUR RESEARCH

During 2017, we surveyed more than 60 international booksellers and book-discovery partners. Our goal was to answer some of the questions we hear from publishers most often:

- What data elements should we focus on to increase sales?
- With limited resources, what elements are most important to enhance?

The objective of the survey was to identify which data elements publishers need to focus on to drive discovery and sales based on what's most relevant to retailers.

With those questions in mind, we crafted our survey, using industry best practices and our own experience, to identify 24 metadata attributes (such as title, contributor, and series) to focus on for our study. We asked retailers a series of multiple choice, open-ended, rank-order scaling, and yes-or-no questions to find out which metadata elements they used, and whether they were being displayed online, used behind the scenes, or not being used at all. We then conducted in-depth interviews with 14 of the sites with the largest global market share in the book industry.

In evaluating the responses to the surveys, we gave a heavier weight to retailers with an outsize percent of market share. So, Barnes & Noble's responses are weighed more heavily than a startup book-discovery site.

Finally, we reviewed the overall response pool to ensure we had adequate representation across the global book market and across retail and book discovery. We distilled the responses from each partner into a profile which, we hope, will serve as a handy reference for you in your metadata and marketing efforts.

PARTICIPANT PROFILE KEY TAKEAWAYS

- Curation: 43.7% of respondents have fewer than 500,000 titles in their current catalog.
- Digital: 60% sell ebooks or other digital products.

DETERMINING TITLES TO CARRY

We've found there's a mixed approach from retailers when determining which titles to carry, with **45.65% of retailers advising other factors than genre, category, format and price are at play.**

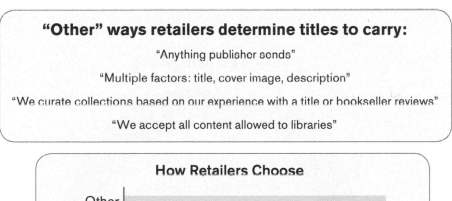

"Other" ways retailers determine titles to carry:

"Anything publisher sends"

"Multiple factors: title, cover image, description"

"We curate collections based on our experience with a title or bookseller reviews"

"We accept all content allowed to libraries"

How Retailers Choose

Other

Price

Format

Category

Genre

not important   very important

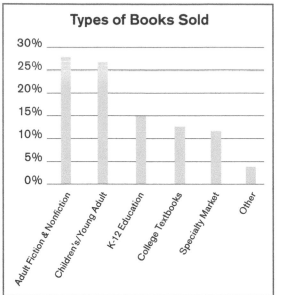

Types of Books Sold

"Other" types of books sold:

"Comics and graphic novels"

"Enhanced ebooks"

"Gift items"

Titles in Current Catalog

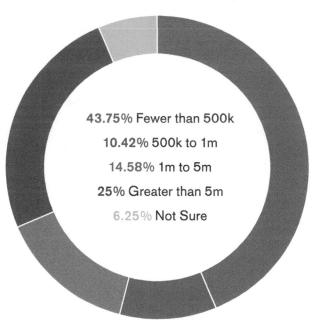

43.75% Fewer than 500k

10.42% 500k to 1m

14.58% 1m to 5m

25% Greater than 5m

6.25% Not Sure

HTML TAGS KEY TAKEAWAYS

53% of retailers utilize HTML Tags

Top 10 HTML Tags Used

1. `<br />`
2. `<br/>`
3. `<br>`
4. `<p>`
5. `<b></b>`
6. `<i></i>`
7. `<ul></ul>`
8. `<li></li>`
9. `<ol></ol>`
10. `<strong></strong>`

Which HTML Tags Are Most Supported?

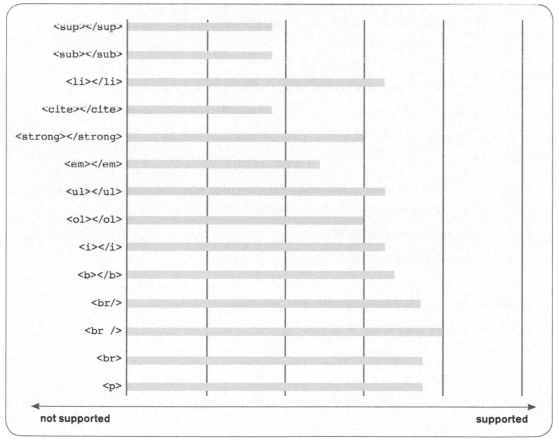

not supported · supported

`<sup></sup>`, `<sub></sub>`, `<li></li>`, `<cite></cite>`, `<strong></strong>`, `<em></em>`, `<ul></ul>`, `<ol></ol>`, `<i></i>`, `<b></b>`, `<br/>`, `<br />`, `<br>`, `<p>`

DIGITAL PRODUCTS TAKEAWAYS

50% of retailers accept **digital pre-orders**.

To sell digital pre-orders, retailers require:

Pub date **85.7%**

Title **85.7%**

Price **85.7%**

On sale date 80.9%

Cover image 76%

File received 8.5%

How retailers manage pre-orders **if the ebook file is not delivered on time**.

Remove from sale 44.4%

Push pub date out 33%

Send alert to publisher/distributor to change date 22%

Push pub date out 16.6 %

When asked, "Do you use **retail price** when no library price is provided," we found:

Yes 46.15%

No 19.23%

Yes, if contractually allowed 19.23%

Not Sure 15.38%

Although **50%** of retailers surveyed **do not use price effective dates**, we found if price effective dates are provided retailers will use the data for:

Onsite merchandising 31%

Promotional price updates 31%

Roadblocks to retailers utilizing price effective dates:

Technical constraints 73%

Inconsistent/inaccurate data 9%

Other 18%

HOW KEY RETAILERS USE METADATA

As part of our research, we arranged follow up interviews with some of the larger, more influential, and innovative online booksellers and discovery engines.

Our goal was to gain a better understanding of how these partners are using certain data elements and what's most relevant to their businesses.

The table in this section outlines the 24 primary data elements and how they're being used by specific retailers, based on survey results and our research. This data is accurate as of July 2017. The screenshots that follow were taken at the time of publication.

	Jet.com	Walmart	Books-A-Million	Aerio	Indigo	Kobo	Above the Treeline
HTML	Y	Y	Y	Y	Y	Y	Y
Product Description	Y	Y	Y	Y	Y	Y	Y
Series Name	I	Y	Y	N	Y	Y	Y
BISAC Subject Code	Y	Y	Y	Y	Y	Y	Y
Related Product	N	N	Y	Y	Y	I	Y
Territory Rights	N	N	Y	N	I	I	Y
BIC Category	N	N	N	N	N	I	Y
Series Number	I	Y	I	N	Y	Y	N
Thema Code	N	N	N	N	I	N	N
Edition Number	I	Y	N	N	Y	Y	Y
Product Form	Y	Y	Y	Y	Y	Y	Y
Product Form Detail	N	N	N	I	Y	I	Y
Audience Code	I	N	I	I	I	I	Y
Age Range	I	Y	Y	N	I	I	Y
Short Description	N	N	Y	I	I	N	Y
Reading Levels	I	Y	Y	N	I	N	Y
Dimensions	I	Y	Y	Y	Y	N	Y
Weight	I	Y	Y	I	I	N	Y
Contributor Bio	I	N	I	N	I	N	Y
Keywords	N	N	I	N	I	I	N
BISAC Regional Theme Code	N	N	N	N	I	N	N
Contributor Place Relator	N	N	N	N	I	N	N
Country of Origin	N	N	N	N	I	N	N
ISNI	N	N	N	N	I	N	N

Y = Accepted (visible to customers)   I = Accepted, but NOT visible to customers   N = No

	Apple	Amazon	Google Play	Barnes & Noble	WHSmith	Waterstones	Booktopia
HTML	Y	Y	Y	Y	Y	Y	Y
Product Description	Y	Y	Y	Y	Y	Y	Y
Series Name	Y	Y	Y	Y	Y	Y	Y
BISAC Subject Code	Y	Y	Y	I	Y	Y	Y
Related Product	I	Y	I	Y	Y	Y	Y
Territory Rights	I	I	I	I	I	N	N
BIC Category	Y	Y	Y	I	N	N	N
Series Number	Y	Y	Y	Y	Y	Y	Y
Thema Code	Y	Y	N	I	N	N	N
Edition Number	N	Y	Y	Y	Y	Y	Y
Product Form	N	Y	I	Y	Y	Y	Y
Product Form Detail	N	I	I	Y	N	N	N
Audience Code	N	I	I	N	N	N	Y
Age Range	N	Y	I	Y	N	N	Y
Short Description	N	I	N	N	N	N	N
Reading Levels	N	I	N	Y	N	N	Y
Dimensions	N	Y	N	Y	N	Y	Y
Weight	N	Y	N	N	Y	Y	Y
Contributor Bio	N	Y	Y	Y	Y	Y	Y
Keywords	N	I	N	Y	N	N	N
BISAC Regional Theme Code	N	Y	N	N	N	N	N
Contributor Place Relator	N	I	N	N	N	N	N
Country of Origin	N	I	N	N	N	N	Y
ISNI	N	N	N	N	N	N	N

Y = Accepted (visible to customers)   I = Accepted, but NOT visible to customers   N = No

Description

The first of a three-part series investigating the wonders of nature by New York Times bestselling author Peter Wohlleben. Watch for Book 2, The Inner Life of Animals Are trees social beings? In this international bestseller, forester and author Peter Wohlleben convincingly makes the case that, yes, the forest is a social network. He draws on groundbreaking scientific discoveries to describe how trees are like human families: tree parents live together with their children, communicate with them, support them as they grow, share nutrients with those who are sick or struggling, and even warn each other of impending dangers. Wohlleben also shares his deep love of woods and forests, explaining the amazing processes of life, death, and regeneration he has observed in his woodland. After learning about the complex life of trees, a walk in the woods will never be the same again.Includes a Note From a Forest Scientist, by Dr. Suzanne SimardPublished in partnership with the David Suzuki Institute

- ISBN13: 9781771642484
- Publisher: Greystone Books
- Publication Year: 2016
- Format: Hardcover
- Pages: 00288

HTML	Y
Product Description	Y
Series Name	I
BISAC Subject Code	Y
Related Product	N
Territory Rights	N
BIC Category	N
Series Number	I
Thema Code	N
Edition Number	I
Product Form	Y
Product Form Detail	N
Audience Code	I
Age Range	I
Short Description	N
Reading Levels	I
Dimensions	I
Weight	I
Contributor Bio	I
Keywords	N
BISAC Regional Theme Code	N
Contributor Place Relator	N
Country of Origin	N
ISNI	N

Y = Accepted (visible to customers)
I = Accepted, but NOT visible to customers
N = No

JET

Location: United States

Business description: Online retailer (owned by Walmart)

Types of books sold:
- Adult Fiction & Nonfiction
- Children's/Young Adult Fiction & Nonfiction
- College Textbooks
- K-12 Education

Titles in catalog: 1m to 5m

Smart Tips

Product description: Keep word count to less than 5,000 or else the title will be systematically blocked from sale.

Importance of BISACs: Up to 3 accepted.

"When a publisher chooses a BISAC code, they're choosing the traffic that will reach the book," says Zarren Kuzma, Manager, Books, at Jet and Walmart. "It's very powerful and very dangerous in that way." Make sure your primary subject code is the most well defined and not a General code. Zarren also emphasizes not to use the subject code Media Tie-in as that can make a book difficult to find online. Remember titles that are in the same family (paperback, hardcover, audio) should also be in the same category. If the Jet team finds a discrepancy between different formats of the same book, they make the call internally as to how a book will be categorized.

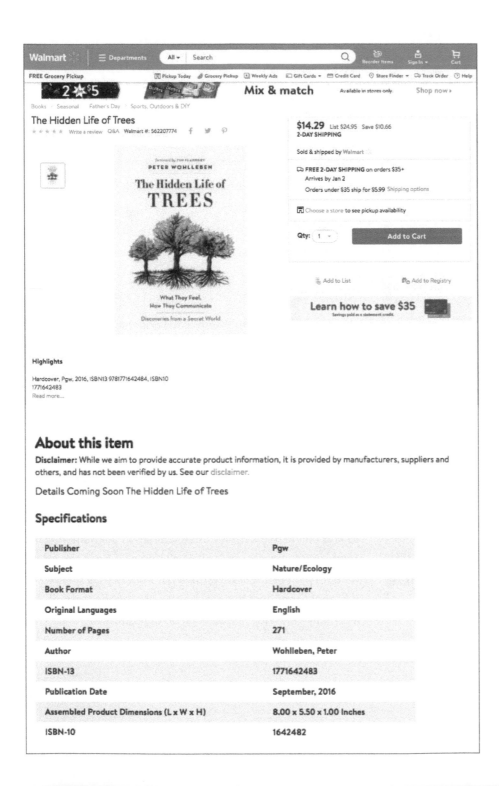

HTML	Y
Product Description	Y
Series Name	Y
BISAC Subject Code	Y
Related Product	N
Territory Rights	N
BIC Category	N
Series Number	Y
Thema Code	N
Edition Number	Y
Product Form	Y
Product Form Detail	N
Audience Code	N
Age Range	Y
Short Description	N
Reading Levels	Y
Dimensions	Y
Weight	Y
Contributor Bio	N
Keywords	N
BISAC Regional Theme Code	N
Contributor Place Relator	N
Country of Origin	N
ISNI	N

Y = Accepted (visible to customers)
I = Accepted, but NOT visible to customers
N = No

WALMART

Location: United States

Business description: Brick and mortar retailer; online retailer

Types of books sold:
- Adult Fiction & Nonfiction
- Children's/Young Adult Fiction & Nonfiction
- College Textbooks

Titles in catalog: 1m to 5m

Smart Tips

Determining titles to carry: Multiple factors are considered, such as title, cover image, and description. That's right: if your book is missing a cover image, it won't be carried at Walmart.com.

Product description: According to Walmart's site analytics, a longer description doesn't contribute to more sales. Walmart has found 5,000 characters is more than sufficient for a product description.

Importance of BISACs: Walmart has just one BISAC flowing into its system, so getting that categorization right is key to consumers discovering the title.

HTML	Y
Product Description	Y
Series Name	Y
BISAC Subject Code	Y
Related Product	Y
Territory Rights	Y
BIC Category	N
Series Number	I
Thema Code	N
Edition Number	N
Product Form	Y
Product Form Detail	N
Audience Code	I
Age Range	Y
Short Description	Y
Reading Levels	Y
Dimensions	Y
Weight	Y
Contributor Bio	I
Keywords	I
BISAC Regional Theme Code	N
Contributor Place Relator	N
Country of Origin	N
ISNI	N

Y = Accepted (visible to customers)
I = Accepted, but NOT visible to customers
N = No

BOOKS-A-MILLION

Location: United States

Business description: Brick and mortar retailer; online retailer; wholesaler

Types of books sold:

- Adult Fiction & Nonfiction
- Children's/Young Adult Fiction & Nonfiction
- K-12 Education

Titles in catalog: 1m to 5m

Smart Tips

Overall Books-A-Million is interested in any data attributes to help make purchase experience easier for consumers.

Determining titles to carry: Largely based on publisher availability.

Pain points: Poorly formatted descriptions or lack of description. Be sure to use HTML market to make your description pop.

BISACs: Up to 3 accepted. Subject codes are displayed in the way the publisher has ordered the information.

Customer recommendations: Algorithm based on consumer purchase data.

foreword by TIM FLANNERY

PETER WOHLLEBEN

The Hidden Life of
TREES

What They Feel,
How They Communicate

Discoveries from a Secret World

The Hidden Life of Trees: What They Feel, How They Communicate-- Discoveries from a Secret World

by Wohlleben, Peter foreword by Flannery, Tim translated by Billinghurst, Jane

CHOOSE A FORMAT

Hardcover	$24.95

Qty: 1   **Add to Cart**

SHARE THIS BOOK

BOOK DETAILS

ISBN: 9781771642484
Publisher: Greystone Books
Format: Hardcover
Publication Date: 09/13/2016
Page Count: 288
Category: Plants - Trees
Category: Essays
Language: English
Dimensions: 1.10" x 5.60" x 7.60"

DESCRIPTION

The first of a three-part series investigating the wonders of nature by *New York Times* bestselling author Peter Wohlleben. Watch for Book 2, *The Inner Life of Animals*

Are trees social beings? In this international bestseller, forester and author Peter Wohlleben convincingly makes the case that, yes, the forest is a social network. He draws on groundbreaking scientific discoveries to describe how trees are like human families: tree parents live together with their children, communicate with them, support them as they grow, share nutrients with those who are sick or struggling, and even warn each other of impending dangers. Wohlleben also shares his deep love of woods and forests, explaining the amazing processes of life, death, and regeneration he has observed in his woodland.

After learning about the complex life of trees, a walk in the woods will never be the same again.

Includes a Note From a Forest Scientist, by Dr.Suzanne Simard

Published in partnership with the David Suzuki Institute

HTML	Y
Product Description	Y
Series Name	N
BISAC Subject Code	Y
Related Product	Y
Territory Rights	N
BIC Category	N
Series Number	N
Thema Code	N
Edition Number	N
Product Form	Y
Product Form Detail	I
Audience Code	I
Age Range	N
Short Description	I
Reading Levels	N
Dimensions	Y
Weight	I
Contributor Bio	N
Keywords	N
BISAC Regional Theme Code	N
Contributor Place Relator	N
Country of Origin	N
ISNI	N

Y = Accepted (visible to customers)
I = Accepted, but NOT visible to customers
N = No

AERIO

Location: United States

Business description: Online retailer

Types of books sold:

- Adult Fiction & Nonfiction
- Children's/Young Adult Fiction & Nonfiction
- K-12 Education

Titles in catalog: Greater than 5m

Smart Tips

Product description: The word limit for a product description is 1,000 words.

BISACs: Aerio displays two BISAC subject codes, with the publisher's designated primary subject code displayed first.

Digital Pre-orders: Accepted with required data:

- Pub date*
- On sale date
- Title
- Cover image
- Price

*If the ebook file is not delivered by the pub date, Aerio will show the title available for pre-order indefinitely until the publisher provides the file.

HTML	Y
Product Description	Y
Series Name	Y
BISAC Subject Code	Y
Related Product	Y
Territory Rights	I
BIC Category	N
Series Number	Y
Thema Code	I
Edition Number	Y
Product Form	Y
Product Form Detail	Y
Audience Code	I
Age Range	I
Short Description	I
Reading Levels	I
Dimensions	Y
Weight	I
Contributor Bio	I
Keywords	I
BISAC Regional Theme Code	I
Contributor Place Relator	I
Country of Origin	I
ISNI	I

Y = Accepted (visible to customers)
I = Accepted, but NOT visible to customers
N = No

INDIGO

Location: Canada

Business description: Brick & mortar retailer; online retailer

Types of books sold:

- Adult Fiction & Nonfiction
- Children's/Young Adult Fiction & Nonfiction

Titles in catalog: 1m to 5m

Smart Tips

ISNI: Indigo is one of the few retailers to embrace ISNI and incorporate it into its data architecture. Indigo will accept ISNI and apply it to your contributor name to ensure he or she doesn't get confused with other contributors with the same name in search results.

Subjects: Indigo's main subject classification scheme is BISAC subject codes. However, it intend's to ramp up use of Thema subject codes, BISAC regional codes, and keywords.

Timing: Indigo strongly encourages publishers and authors to provide key metadata 180 days prior to pub date to boost pre-orders.

HTML	Y
Product Description	Y
Series Name	Y
BISAC Subject Code	Y
Related Product	I
Territory Rights	I
BIC Category	I
Series Number	Y
Thema Code	N
Edition Number	Y
Product Form	Y
Product Form Detail	I
Audience Code	I
Age Range	I
Short Description	N
Reading Levels	N
Dimensions	N
Weight	N
Contributor Dio	N
Keywords	I
BISAC Regional Theme Code	N
Contributor Place Relator	N
Country of Origin	N
ISNI	N

Y = Accepted (visible to customers)
I = Accepted, but NOT visible to customers
N = No

KOBO

Location: Canada

Business description: Ebook only retailer

Types of books sold:

- Adult Fiction & Nonfiction
- Children's/Young Adult Fiction & Nonfiction
- College Textbooks
- K-12 Education
- Specialty Market

Titles in catalog: Greater than 5 m

Smart Tips

Product description: There is no word limit for the product description.

BISACs/BIC: There is a limit of 3 BISAC subject codes and/or BIC categories accepted. Up to 3 are displayed to consumers and used to map titles to specific categories. BISACs/BIC are reviewed internally to limit certain content such as erotica from the catalog.

Related product: Although Kobo only sells digital content, the related product data is used internally and sent to partners like Indigo to show ebook formats available for consumers.

Digital pre-orders: Accepted with required data:

- Pub date*
- On sale date
- Title
- Price

*If the ebook file is not delivered on time, Kobo will send an alert to the publisher/distributor to change the pub date.

Home | Publishers | Catalogs | Buzz | Review Copies | Reviews | People | Shelves | Tags | Orders | Event Grids

• 3 Active Community ▼

Back to List   ◀ 1 of 2 ▶

✓ 1. Greystone Books   Ingram Publisher Services

The Hidden Life of Trees: What They Feel, How They Communicate—Discoveries from a Secret World ✕
Peter Wohlleben, Tim Flannery (Foreword by), Jane Billinghurst (T..
BACKLIST | On Sale Date: September 13, 2016, Ship Date: August 22, 2016
9781771642484, 1771642483
Hardcover
$24.95 USD, £16.99 GBP, €18.99 EUR
Discount Code: HC
Nature / Plants / Trees

288 pages
B&W illustrations
7.5 in H | 5.3 in W | 0.9 lb Wt
Sales Rights: View
Honors ▦

📖 Featured Reviews   1   Community Reviews
16   Much Love!   3   Community Shelves
0   Comments
Goodreads:
👥 Peers: Checked Out in 76% • On Hand in 58% • On Order in 16%

Add Category 📍
EA Demo Library - ...
Carton Qty: 20

Images ▲

Content ▲   Comps (10) ▼   Related (2) ▼   Refs ▼   Review 💬 | Shelf 🔖 | Note ✏ | Tags 🏷 ♡ ◁ ⋯

Summary ▲ ∞

The first of a three-part series investigating the wonders of nature by *New York Times* bestselling author Peter Wohlleben. Book two, *The Inner Life of Animals*, is now available as well.

Are trees social beings? In this international bestseller, forester and author Peter Wohlleben convincingly makes the case that, yes, the forest is a social network. He draws on groundbreaking scientific discoveries to describe how trees are like human families: tree parents live together with their children, communicate with them, support them as they grow, share nutrients with those who are sick or struggling, and even warn each other of impending dangers. Wohlleben also shares his deep love of woods and forests, explaining the amazing processes of life, death, and regeneration he has observed in his woodland.

After learning about the complex life of trees, a walk in the woods will never be the same again.

Includes a Note From a Forest Scientist, by Dr.Suzanne Simard

Contributor Bio(s) ▲ ∞

Peter Wohlleben spent over twenty years working for the forestry commission in Germany before leaving to put his ideas of ecology into practice. He now runs an environmentally-friendly woodland in Germany, where he is working for the return of primeval forests. He is the author of numerous books about trees.

▼ **Related Products**

Related Products

Name	ISBN	Price	Type	Format	Pub Date
Ebooks					
The Hidden Life of Trees	9781771642491	$24.99 USD	Publisher_Derived	E-Book	9/13/2016

HTML	Y
Product Description	Y
Series Name	Y
BISAC Subject Code	Y
Related Product	Y
Territory Rights	Y
BIC Category	Y
Series Number	N
Thema Code	N
Edition Number	Y
Product Form	Y
Product Form Detail	Y
Audience Code	Y
Age Range	Y
Short Description	Y
Reading Levels	Y
Dimensions	Y
Weight	Y
Contributor Bio	Y
Keywords	N
BISAC Regional Theme Code	N
Contributor Place Relator	N
Country of Origin	N
ISNI	N

Y = Accepted (visible to customers)
I = Accepted, but NOT visible to customers
N = No

ABOVE THE TREELINE (EDELWEISS)

Location: United States

Business description: Metadata aggregation/
distribution; software developer/IT consultancy;
digital services supplier
Titles in catalog: 1m to 5m

Smart Tips

Comparable title data: It's very important to include
this information in Edelweiss for stores and libraries
making frontlist purchase planning decisions.

Contributor bio: Highly recommended to provide
additional data about the author.

BISACs/BIC: There is a limit of 3 BISAC subject codes
and/or BIC categories accepted per title. These
categories are displayed in the catalog in the same
order the publisher sends the data.

Ancillary marketing metadata accepted:

- Videos
- Excerpts
- Book reviews
- Advertisements
- Links
- Honors/awards

The Hidden Life of Trees

What They Feel, How They Communicate Discoveries from a Secret World

Peter Wohlleben & Tim Flannery

View More by This Author

This book can be downloaded and read in iBooks on your Mac or iOS device.

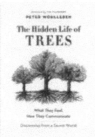

View on iBooks

$16.99

Available on iPhone, iPad, iPod touch, and Mac.

Category: Nature
Published: **Sep 13, 2016**
Publisher: **Greystone Books**
Seller: The Perseus Books Group, LLC
Print Length: 288 Pages
Language: English

Requirements: To view this book, you must have an iOS device with iBooks 1.3.1 or later and iOS 4.3.3 or later, or a Mac with iBooks 1.0 or later and OS X 10.9 or later.

Customer Ratings

★★★★½ 43 Ratings

More by Peter Wohlleben & Tim Flannery

The Inner Life of Animals

Description

In *The Hidden Life of Trees*, Peter Wohlleben shares his deep love of woods and forests and explains the amazing processes of life, death, and regeneration he has observed in the woodland and the amazing scientific processes behind the wonders of which we are blissfully unaware. Much like human families, tree parents live together with their children, communicate with them, and support them as they grow, sharing nutrients with those who are sick or struggling and creating an ecosystem that mitigates the impact of extremes of heat and cold for the whole group. As a result of such interactions, trees in a family or community are protected and can live to be very old. In contrast, solitary trees, like street kids, have a tough time of it and in most cases die much earlier than those in a group.

Drawing on groundbreaking new discoveries, Wohlleben presents the science behind the secret and
...More

From Publishers Weekly

Jul 25, 2016 - This fascinating book will intrigue readers who love a walk through the woods. Wohlleben, who worked for the German forestry commission for 20 years and now manages a beech forest in Germany, has gathered research from scientists around the world examining how trees communicate and interact with one another. They do so using a variety of methods, including the secretion of scents and sound vibrations to warn neighboring plants of potential attacks by insects and hungry herbivores, drought, and other dangers. The book includes a note from forest scientist Suzanne Simard of the University of British Columbia, whose studies showed that entire forests can be connected by "using chemical signals sent through the fungal networks around their root tips" and led to the term "the wood-wide web." Wohlleben anthropomorphizes his subject, using such terms as friendship and parenting, which serves to make the technical information relatable, and he backs up his
...More

Customer Reviews

The Secret Life of Trees ★★★★
by Paulofgc

Beautifully written by a naturalist who is both scientist and lover of nature. The secrets Peter Wohlleben reveal should be known by all. Readers will never look at trees or forests the same again. Fascinating journey into a world we all thought we knew well, but actually did not know at all.

Just beautiful ★★★★★
by soccerqueen13

What a wonderful read. I will be reading more by this man. He has woken up a whole new world for me.

Customers Also Bought

| The Invention of... | Lab Girl | The Soul of an O... | H Is for Hawk | The Genius of Bi... |
| Andrea Wulf | Hope Jahren | Sy Montgomery | Helen MacDon... | Jennifer Acker... |

HTML	Y
Product Description	Y
Series Name	Y
BISAC Subject Code	Y
Related Product	I
Territory Rights	I
BIC Category	Y
Series Number	Y
Thema Code	Y
Edition Number	N
Product Form	N
Product Form Detail	N
Audience Code	N
Age Range	N
Short Description	N
Reading Levels	N
Dimensions	N
Weight	N
Contributor Bio	N
Keywords	N
BISAC Regional Theme Code	N
Contributor Place Relator	N
Country of Origin	N
ISNI	N

Y = Accepted (visible to customers)
I = Accepted, but NOT visible to customers
N = No

APPLE

Location: United States

Business description: Ebook only retailer

Types of books sold:

- Adult Fiction & Nonfiction
- Children's/Young Adult Fiction & Nonfiction
- College Textbooks
- K-12 Education

Titles in catalog: 1m to 5m

Smart Tips

Product description: The word limit for product descriptions is 4,000 characters, and it's recommended to utilize a nongeneric description or it may be rejected in Apple's system.

BISACs: Although Apple accepts an unlimited number of BISACS, they only show 1 to consumers and prefer a maximum of 3 to be sent. If the content is of an erotic nature, Apple highly recommends including this as the first BISAC code or the title could be suppressed from sale.

Digital pre-orders: Powerful driver of sales at Apple and are accepted with the below required data:

- Pub date*
- Title
- On sale date
- Price

*If the ebook file is not delivered on time, Apple will remove the title from sale.

Series: Including the series name and number is essential information for Apple to use in the future to create collections for consumers to browse an entire series at once.

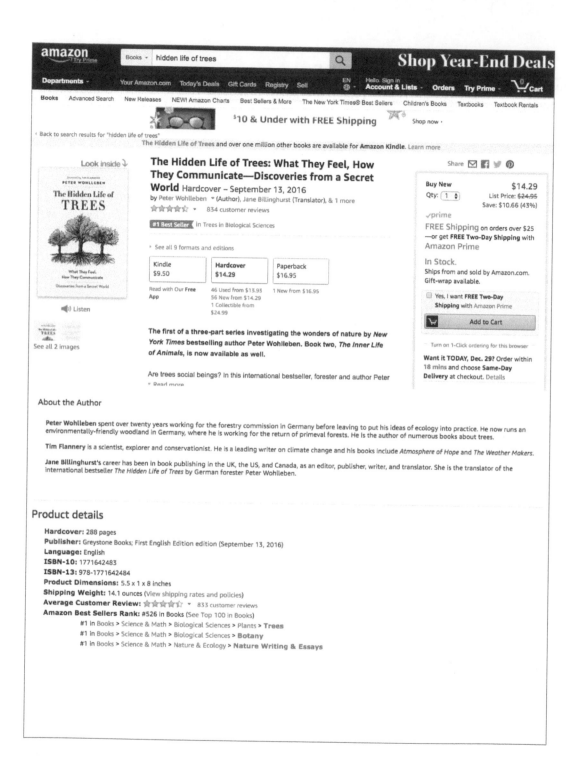

HTML	Y
Product Description	Y
Series Name	Y
BISAC Subject Code	Y
Related Product	Y
Territory Rights	I
BIC Category	Y
Series Number	Y
Thema Code	Y
Edition Number	Y
Product Form	Y
Product Form Detail	I
Audience Code	I
Age Range	Y
Short Description	I
Reading Levels	I
Dimensions	Y
Weight	Y
Contributor Bio	Y
Keywords	I
BISAC Regional Theme Code	Y
Contributor Place Relator	I
Country of Origin	I
ISNI	N

Y = Accepted (visible to customers)
I = Accepted, but NOT visible to customers
N = No

AMAZON

Location: United States

Business description: Online retailer

Types of books sold:

- Adult Fiction & Nonfiction
- Children's/Young Adult Fiction & Nonfiction
- College Textbooks
- K-12 Education
- Specialty Market

Titles in catalog: Greater than 5m

Smart Tips

Keywords: Highly recommended to include to help consumers easily discover your title, since keywords can boost placement in search results on site. Amazon will accept up to 97 keywords.

Product description: Word limit for product description is 4,000 characters, and it's recommended to utilize HTML markup within the description.

Author pages: Contributor biographical and contributor place relator information is being applied on Amazon to bring readers closer to authors and other works they've published.

Series: Including the series name and number is essential information for Amazon to appropriately link titles for consumers who may be interested in seeing and buying all the books in an ordered series from the same page.

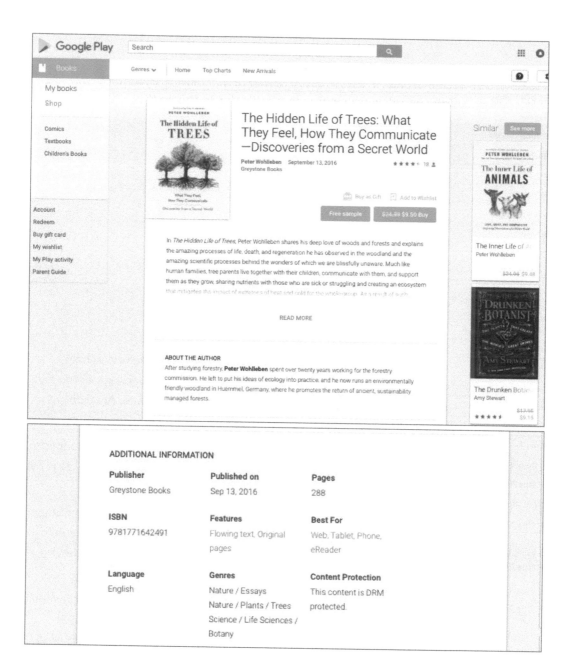

ADDITIONAL INFORMATION

Publisher
Greystone Books

Published on
Sep 13, 2016

Pages
288

ISBN
9781771642491

Features
Flowing text, Original
pages

Best For
Web, Tablet, Phone,
eReader

Language
English

Genres
Nature / Essays
Nature / Plants / Trees
Science / Life Sciences /
Botany

Content Protection
This content is DRM
protected.

HTML	Y
Product Description	Y
Series Name	Y
BISAC Subject Code	Y
Related Product	I
Territory Rights	I
BIC Category	Y
Series Number	Y
Thema Code	N
Edition Number	Y
Product Form	I
Product Form Detail	I
Audience Code	I
Age Range	I
Short Description	N
Reading Levels	N
Dimensions	N
Weight	N
Contributor Bio	Y
Keywords	N
BISAC Regional Theme Code	N
Contributor Place Relator	N
Country of Origin	N
ISNI	N

Y = Accepted (visible to customers)
I = Accepted, but NOT visible to customers
N = No

GOOGLE PLAY

Location: United States

Business description: Ebook only retailer

Types of books sold:

- Adult Fiction & Nonfiction
- Children's/Young Adult Fiction & Nonfiction
- College Textbooks
- K-12 Education

Titles in catalog: 1m to 5m

Smart Tips

Product description: While there is no word limit for a long description, Google allows an estimated 350 characters for the short description.

Misleading content: As a policy, Google doesn't permit metadata that is "confusingly similar" to other works. This includes misleading titles, authors, descriptions, and covers.

Digital pre-orders: Accepted with required data:

- On sale date*
- Title
- Price

*If the ebook file is not delivered on time, Google will remove the title from sale.

HTML	Y
Product Description	Y
Series Name	Y
BISAC Subject Code	I
Related Product	Y
Territory Rights	I
BIC Category	I
Series Number	Y
Thema Code	I
Edition Number	Y
Product Form	Y
Product Form Detail	Y
Audience Code	N
Age Range	Y
Short Description	N
Reading Levels	Y
Dimensions	Y
Weight	N
Contributor Bio	Y
Keywords	Y
BISAC Regional Theme Code	N
Contributor Place Relator	N
Country of Origin	N
ISNI	N

Y = Accepted (visible to customers)
I = Accepted, but NOT visible to customers
N = No

BARNES & NOBLE

Location: United States

Business description: Brick & mortar retailer; online retailer

Types of books sold:

- Adult Fiction & Nonfiction
- Children's/Young Adult Fiction & Nonfiction
- College Textbooks
- K-12 Education
- Specialty Market

Titles in catalog: Unknown

Smart Tips

Keywords: Barnes & Noble has started accepting limited keywords. We expect they will expand their range of acceptable keywords in the near future, so keep sending them their way!

Sales rank: Barnes & Noble incorporates a sales rank into each title's product details. This can be helpful for you to understand where your book is stacking up.

Lexile: Barnes & Noble will take Lexile codes you provide them to display reading levels and comprehension for your title.

The Hidden Life of Trees: What They Feel, How They Communicate-Discoveries from a Secret World

By: Peter Wohlleben *(Author)*, Tim Flannery *(Foreword_author)*

Hardback

MORE THAN 4 WEEKS

Quantity 1

£16.99

& FREE Saver Delivery on orders over £20

ADD TO BASKET

DESCRIPTION

"A paradigm-smashing chronicle of joyous entanglement that will make you acknowledge your own entanglement in the ancient and ever-new web of being."—Charles Foster, author of Being a Beast Are trees social beings? In this international bestseller, forester and author Peter Wohlleben convincingly makes the case that, yes, the forest is a social network. He draws on groundbreaking scientific discoveries to describe how trees are like human families; tree parents live together with their children, communicate with them, support them as they grow, share nutrients with those who are sick or struggling, and even warn each other of impending dangers. Wohlleben also shares his deep love of woods and forests, explaining the amazing processes of life, death, and regeneration he has observed in his woodland. After learning about the complex life of trees, a walk in the woods will never be the same again. Includes a Note From a

CREATE A REVIEW

There are currently no reviews found for this product. Be the first to review this product.

ABOUT AUTHOR

Peter Wohlleben spent over twenty years working for the forestry commission in Germany before leaving to put his ideas of ecology into practice. He now runs an environmentally-friendly woodland in Germany, where he is working for the return of primeval forests. He is the author of numerous books about trees. Tim Flannery is a scientist, explorer and conservationist. He is a leading writer on climate change and his books include Atmosphere of Hope and The Weather Makers.

PRODUCT DETAILS

DELIVERY INFORMATION

Publication Date:	13/09/2016
ISBN13:	9781771642484
Format:	Hardback
Number Of Pages:	288
ID:	9781771642484
Weight:	414
ISBN10:	1771642483

MORE LIKE THIS

Category: Trees, Wildflowers and Plants »

Category: Natural History »

Category: Books »

Publisher: Greystone Books,Canada »

Imprint: Greystone Books,Canada »

TREES, WILDFLOWERS AND PLANTS

The Wild Flower Key: How to Identify Wild Plants, Trees and Shrubs in Britain and Ireland

Francis Rose

Paperback

In Stock

£17.00 ADD

RRP: £25.00
You save £8.00 (32%)

Food for Free (Collins Gem New edition)

Richard Mabey

Paperback

In Stock

£2.49 ADD

RRP: £4.99
You save £2.50 (50%)

A Natural History of the Hedgerow: And Ditches, Dykes and Dry Stone Walls (Main)

John Wright, John Davey

Hardback

In Stock

£12.24 ADD

RRP: £18.00
You save £5.76 (32%)

HTML	Y
Product Description	Y
Series Name	Y
BISAC Subject Code	Y
Related Product	Y
Territory Rights	I
BIC Category	N
Series Number	Y
Thema Code	N
Edition Number	Y
Product Form	Y
Product Form Detail	N
Audience Code	N
Age Range	N
Short Description	N
Reading Levels	N
Dimensions	N
Weight	Y
Contributor Bio	Y
Keywords	N
BISAC Regional Theme Code	N
Contributor Place Relator	N
Country of Origin	N
ISNI	N

Y = Accepted (visible to customers)
I = Accepted, but NOT visible to customers
N = No

WHSMITH

Location: United Kingdom

Business description: Brick & mortar retailer; online retailer

Types of books sold:

- Adult Fiction & Nonfiction
- Children's/Young Adult Fiction & Nonfiction
- College Textbooks
- K-12 Education
- Specialty Market

Titles in catalog: Unknown

Smart Tips

Nielsen metadata: WHSmith receives their metadata from a supplier called Nielsen Book Data. Publishers pay a fee to Nielsen to have many of their metadata elements distributed to WHSmith and other booksellers. If you notice your metadata at WHSmith isn't as robust as you were expecting, it's probably because you aren't participating in their service.

Thema: WHSmith relies on Thema codes for categorization, though they do also accept BISAC codes.

Awards: WHSmith does quite a bit of merchandising on their site based on awards. If your title has won an award, make sure to include that in your metadata to make it eligible for any site promotions or merchandising.

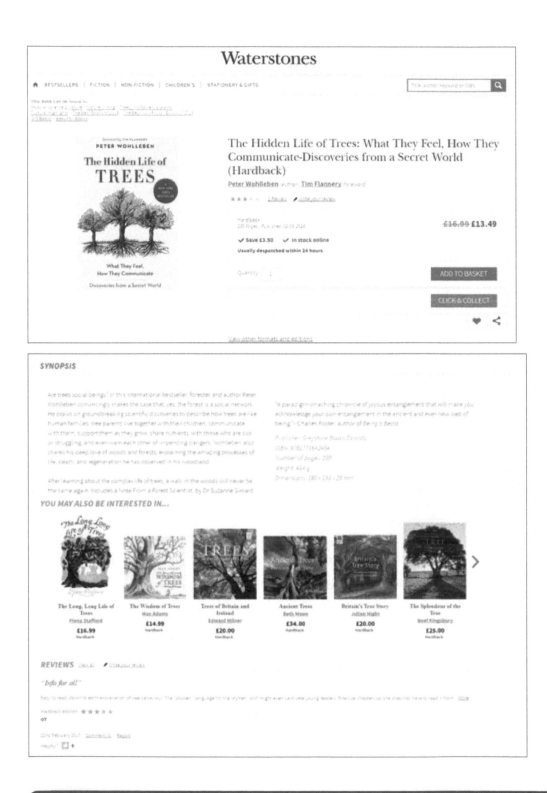

HTML	Y
Product Description	Y
Series Name	Y
BISAC Subject Code	Y
Related Product	Y
Territory Rights	N
BIC Category	N
Series Number	Y
Thema Code	N
Edition Number	Y
Product Form	Y
Product Form Detail	N
Audience Code	N
Age Range	N
Short Description	N
Reading Levels	N
Dimensions	Y
Weight	Y
Contributor Bio	Y
Keywords	N
BISAC Regional Theme Code	N
Contributor Place Relator	N
Country of Origin	N
ISNI	N

Y = Accepted (visible to customers)
I = Accepted, but NOT visible to customers
N = No

WATERSTONES

Location: United Kingdom

Business description: Brick & mortar retailer; online retailer

Types of books sold:

- Adult Fiction & Nonfiction
- Children's/Young Adult Fiction & Nonfiction
- K-12 Education
- Specialty Market

Titles in catalog: Unknown

Smart Tips

Author pages: High-profile authors may receive author pages on the Waterstones website, listing extended biographies and their titles.

Nielsen metadata: Like WHSmith, Waterstones receives its metadata from a supplier called Nielsen Book Data. Publishers pay a fee to Nielsen to have many of their metadata elements distributed to Waterstones and other booksellers. If you notice your metadata at Waterstones isn't as robust as you were expecting, it's probably because you aren't participating in their service.

Pre-orders: Waterstones offers pre-orders of ebooks and print books. Be sure to enable distribution of your metadata prior to your book's on-sale date to capture pre-orders.

HTML	Y
Product Description	Y
Series Name	Y
BISAC Subject Code	Y
Related Product	Y
Territory Rights	N
BIC Category	N
Series Number	Y
Thema Code	N
Edition Number	Y
Product Form	Y
Product Form Detail	N
Audience Code	Y
Age Range	Y
Short Description	N
Reading Levels	Y
Dimensions	Y
Weight	Y
Contributor Bio	Y
Keywords	N
BISAC Regional Theme Code	N
Contributor Place Relator	N
Country of Origin	Y
ISNI	N

Y = Accepted (visible to customers)
I = Accepted, but NOT visible to customers
N = No

BOOKTOPIA

Location: Australia

Business description: Online retailer

Types of books sold:

- Adult Fiction & Nonfiction
- Children's/Young Adult Fiction & Nonfiction
- College Textbooks
- K-12 Education
- Specialty Market

Titles in catalog: Unknown

Smart Tips

Contributor bio: Booktopia only displays the contributor bio for the primary author. Keep this in mind when deciding which contributor bios to send out. Booktopia also has dedicated author pages for these contributors.

Pre-orders: Booktopia offers pre-orders of books and merchandises top pre-orders on its site. Be sure to enable distribution of your metadata prior to your book's on sale date to capture pre-orders of your print and ebooks.

CHAPTER 4: Metadata & Libraries

Libraries present unique demands for metadata, and making your book discoverable in a library setting requires some adjustments to the marketplace model. In this chapter, we'll explore ways to strengthen metadata to serve libraries and their patrons, and you'll learn about the potential for increasing your book's visibility through well-placed reviews in library journals.

A library thrives on organization. Anyone who strolls into a library expects to be able to find exactly what they want in a short amount of time, particularly in an age when they can simply pull up their phone, tap in a few letters, and have their desired novel delivered to them that same day.

In addition to all of the elements listed in Chapter 2, there are several specific metadata points that are worth expanding on with libraries in mind. These include:

- BISAC codes and library classification schemes
- Age range and complexity
- Cover art and images
- Series name and number
- Author and contributor data
- Product form

In this section we'll further examine these metadata elements and show you how to utilize their strengths to boost discoverability in a library setting. We'll also take an in-depth look at several leading library journals and discuss how having your titles reviewed by each is a great method to increase visibility. We're going to focus primarily on public libraries and not on academic or school libraries because of the more nuanced requirements for those audiences.

Finally, we'll examine some exclusive publisher metadata insights from Ingram's Collection Development team about how lack of focus in certain data elements can lead to inconsistent and incomplete metadata for both libraries and their patrons.

LIBRARY METADATA ESSENTIALS

Unlike online bookstores, which (thanks to metadata!) can "stock" unlimited quantities of books through a virtual distribution network without physically shelving any of them, libraries must purchase all of their books before presenting them to patrons. Library success typically is measured by the number of checkouts or circulation of materials. Therefore it's important for a library to build a collection of books that will be circulated and can easily be found by a patron. In general, libraries require substantially more metadata than retailers in order to inform their purchasing decision and also to ensure books are cataloged in a way that they are easily accessed by patrons.

BISAC Codes and Library Classification Schemes

BISAC SUBJECT CODES

If you are unfamiliar with **BISAC subject codes**, please visit the BISAC section of Chapter 2 in this book. Librarians and wholesalers may use BISAC codes to help build their book collections. There are several important tips regarding BISACs for libraries in particular:

1. Ensure consistency across various formats/product forms and channels (such as iPage and Edelweiss). Inconsistency can lead to patron confusion and catalog disorganization.

2. Consider using 4 or 5 BISAC subject codes instead of the usual recommended 3.

3. Pay extra attention to the relevancy and specificity of the BISAC codes you are assigning to a book. Remember that it is essential for a patron to be able to find the book they want, and they expect to go to a specific shelf and find it there. Improper or overly general BISAC codes within libraries can lead to significant catalog confusion or may result in your book being excluded from library collections.

A common problem in BISAC codes for libraries is the overuse of the *General Fiction* code (*FIC000000*). As noted in our earlier discussion of BISAC, there is almost always a better, more specific choice. If you have written or published books with general fiction BISACs, make it a priority to reassign them to more relevant subjects. The good news is that a library's complex organization system allows you the luxury of additional subject codes to better define and categorize the book.

DEWEY CATEGORIES AND NUMBERS

The **Dewey Decimal Classification** system is used widely by libraries, especially for nonfiction books. Dewey numbers are considered an important piece of metadata within libraries in relation to organization and even certain elements of audience age. Whereas the term metadata has only become increasingly popular just over the past two decades, the Dewey Decimal Classification system is a type of metadata that predates our modern computers and data systems by over 100 years.

Dewey numbers are structured hierarchically, similar to Thema schemes. An upper-level number can be refined further and further with additional numbers, as demonstrated below:

- *600 Technology*
- *630 Agriculture and related technologies*
- *636 Animal husbandry*
- *636.7 Dogs*
- *636.8 Cats*

Each topic is derived from 10 main classes:

- *000 Computer science, information & general works*
- *100 Philosophy & psychology*
- *200 Religion*
- *300 Social sciences*
- *400 Language*
- *500 Science*
- *600 Technology*
- *700 Arts & recreation*
- *800 Literature*
- *900 History & geography*

These classes are broken down into what is called the hundred **divisions** (a new division every 10 numbers within 000 to 990) and then further broken down into the thousand **sections** (a new section every number from 000 to 999). The full list of divisions and sections can be found on the Dewey Services website (oclc.org/en/dewey/features/summaries.html) under their second and third summaries.

There are two special characters that you may sometimes see in the Dewey code field that are related to age range:

"E": Easy fiction

- Indicates fiction books intended for children grade 3/age 8 or younger

"Fic": Fiction

- Indicates fiction books intended for children above grade 3/age 8, including young adult and high school age

These two codes are not meant to serve as a replacement for other methods of indicating audience age with metadata. Always use the standard methods for audience age in conjunction with these if using Dewey.

Dewey numbers may be used in conjunction with BISAC codes. It is not necessary to choose one classification system or the other. However, in general, the Dewey system is used more broadly than BISAC subject codes among libraries.

LIBRARY OF CONGRESS SUBJECT HEADINGS

The Library of Congress has developed its own system of subject headings, called the **LCSH** (Library of Congress Subject Headings) that is used to catalog books within the Library of Congress. The LCSH is comprehensive and broad based, serving as a thesaurus of subject headings for books and other media. It's referenced all around the world and throughout U.S. libraries, so it's important to understand this system of categorization and be able to utilize it yourself.

LCSH is categorized under either LC Subject Headings or LC Children's Subject Headings, with the following subdivisions (called "concept types") nested underneath:

- Topic: Subdivided based on general topic (e.g. growing media; Roman influences; home care; Buddhist authors)

- Genre Form: Subdivided based on the product form or genre (e.g. pamphlets; biography; sheet music categorized by instrumentation)

- Temporal: Subdivided based on the time period of the content within the book

- Geographic: Subdivided based on geographic location

- Language: Subdivided based on the language of the materials

- Other smaller subdivisions such as "complex subject," "family name," "corporate name," "personal name," etc.

LCSH are physically published in 10 large volumes. Due to the large number of subjects within LCSH and the general nature of their subdivisions, we recommend reviewing and searching through them via the online portal at id.loc.gov.

Age Range and Complexity

The more information you can provide to libraries about your audience, the more hands your books will be placed in. Omitting age range and reading level or providing inaccurate audience guidance immediately shrinks its audience and cuts it off from a huge portion of potential readers.

ACCURACY IN AGE RANGE

Assigning a proper age range requires taking the entire book into account (reading level, content appropriateness, etc.) and assigning a precise age range that truthfully relays such helpful information to patrons. While this is important in the marketplace, it's doubly important for libraries seeking to acquire and circulate a collection of age-appropriate material.

Remember these tips when deciding the proper age range for a book with libraries in mind:

- The reading level of a book should not go beyond the complexity of words used.
- Accuracy should trump current marketplace positioning.

UNDERSTANDING PROMINENT COMPLEXITY RATINGS AND READING PROGRAMS

Various reading programs have been developed, primarily for children, that help to better categorize content based on readability level and provide kids with books targeted to their specific needs or reading skills.

Metadata on text complexity and reading programs can be communicated via the complexity scheme identifier code codelist (List 32).

Text Complexity Scoring

Lexile is a comprehensive framework used exclusively within education to assign reading levels for books. Rather than examining books on an individual basis to define reading level according to themes or other unique materials, Lexile factors its scores based solely on individual words and sentence length. Lexile measurements assess the complexity of written words and provide a gauge that can then be utilized to structure a reading program or other forms of categorization. Lexile is used across a wide variety of reading programs.

Below are the 7 **Lexile codes** that are communicated by Lexile using their **Lexile scores** and **Lexile measurements**. Not all books receive one of the codes below—some simply are scored based on their reading level.

AD: Adult-directed
- Picture books or children's books to be read to children by an adult

NC: Non-conforming
- Books scoring higher than the average for their intended reading age

HL: High-low
- Books scoring below the average for their intended reading age

IG: Illustrated guide
- Picture books where words are secondary

GN: Graphic novel

BR: Beginning reader
- Any book that has a Lexile score lower than 0

NP: Non-prose
- Books that have very little prose and therefore cannot be given a Lexile score

You can learn more about the Lexile framework on their website (lexile.com). Always keep in mind that Lexile determines reading level comprehension based on word and sentence structure alone (quantitative). Other methods of text complexity rating, such as ATOS, take qualitative attributes (themes, etc.) into account as well, and these methods are generally recommended when determining reading levels for older children.

Numerous detailed reading programs utilize the Lexile measurements, and you can find a complete list of programs using Lexile at lexile.com/about-lexile/how-to-get-lexile-measures/readingprograms/.

Specific metadata points to collect for Lexile are:

- Lexile code
- Lexile code description
- Lexile text measure

ATOS (Advantage–TASA Open Standard; Developed by Renaissance) is similar to Lexile but factors in qualitative elements as well, such as levels of meaning, structure, language conventionality, clarity, and knowledge demands. Used in conjunction with Accelerated Reader, ATOS also factors in interest level and genre, taking into account more factors than Lexile tends to, including separate statistics and elements of fiction vs nonfiction.

ATOS is the first formula to include statistics from actual book reading (over 30,000 students, reading almost 1,000,000 books) in addition to data based on short text passages.

Both ATOS and Lexile have pros and cons, so when deciding between the two, it's important to view both options in depth. You can view more details about ATOS on the Renaissance website (renaissance.com/products/practice/accelerated-reader-360/atos-and-text-complexity/).

Recommended Reading Programs

The **Accelerated Reader** is educational software developed for grades K-12. The program follows a very specific flow to guide a reader and determine their reading level, providing them with books that best suit them. The program involves:

- STAR (Standardized Test for the Assessment of Reading) testing to determine reading level
- Use of ATOS to determine a book's complexity level
- Computer quizzes to further determine reading level
- Reporting for a student's parents and teachers

Specific metadata points to collect for the Accelerated Reader program are:

- Accelerated Reader Interest Level
- Accelerated Interest Level Description
- Accelerated Reader Point Value
- Accelerated Reader Quiz Name
- Accelerated Reader Quiz Number
- Accelerated Reader Reading Level (ATOS)

The **Scholastic Guided Reading Program** is a conjoined effort between Scholastic and Fountas & Pinnell to provide a complete reading program solution for students within the classroom setting. Guided Reading focuses on contexts of varying size, ranging from whole class to individual settings, and provides hands-on guidance for teachers to instruct their students and lead them through reading sessions.

The program is divided into 4 "instructional contexts," each with different purposes:

Whole-class instruction
- Interactive read-aloud
- Phonics, spelling, and language instruction

Small-group instruction (heterogeneous groups)
- Book clubs/literature discussion

Small-group instruction (homogeneous groups)
- Guided reading

Individual instruction

- Independent reading
- Conferring

Specific metadata points to collect for the Guided Reading program are:

- Guided Reading Level
- Guided Reading Level Description
- Scholastic Interest Level
- Scholastic Reading Level

One last program to consider is the **Reading Recovery** program. The Reading Recovery program is for children aged 5 or 6 (first grade within the US) that have proven to be slower readers than others in their age range. This is an international program that helps to get those identified as slower readers back on track with a more focused and controlled curriculum. It is considered a "short-term intervention" that pairs specially trained teachers with struggling students. The teachers "work individually with students in daily 30-minute lessons lasting 12 to 20 weeks."

The success rate, according to Reading Recovery, rests at about 75% of those who go through the program. More information can be found at ReadingRecovery.org.

Cover Art and Images

Whether it's within the computer-based catalog or on display on physical shelves, the **jacket** or **cover art** is always the first thing that grabs a patron's attention. Moreover, a digital book without a cover image is often a dealbreaker for a library. For this reason, all digital records should be represented with proper cover art.

The recommended specifications for all digitally stored cover art are as follows:

- JPG or PNG
- 1.6:1 dimension
- Minimum 1563 x 2500 pixels, maximum 10000 x 10000 pixels
- Minimum 72 DPI (dots per inch)
- Maximum 50mb file size
- RGB color profile

Cover art that meets these requirements should be vibrant and easily recognizable at quick glance, no matter what device is used to view it. This helps avoid the problem of blurry cover art. Keep in mind that each catalog system may have different specifications that either exceed or fall short of the above recommendations. In these cases, going with the specifications outlined by the particular catalog is necessary.

For consistency across catalog records and physical stock, the cover art sent with the metadata should match any cover art on the physical book. This is especially helpful in avoiding confusion between editions or books within the same series that may have nearly identical art.

Cover art should always be provided immediately upon putting a book into a catalog or into the distribution process. Lack of art initially can lead to delays.

Series Name and Number

Consistency throughout all data is important, but there are a couple of areas within libraries that require a more intensive focus. The first of these is series. **If a patron is searching for one book in a series (either one they've read previously or one they're interested in), they will expect to the see the other books in the series.** Any experience different from this will cause confusion and may negatively impact circulation. This applies across all subjects: fantasy novels, textbooks, research reports, etc. The proper accuracy in series name and number is crucial.

Please note that a series number is only necessary for series that follow a specific order.

Author and Contributor Data

AUTHOR CONSISTENCY AND DISAMBIGUATION

A clean set of author data (and, for that matter, data for all accounted-for contributors) is invaluable. The most important goals here are consistency and disambiguation.

Consistency between different contributors goes beyond just ensuring that, across all of his novels, "Stephen King" is always spelled as "Stephen King" and not "Steven King" or "S. King." Any additional entries of "Steven King" or "S. King" will split his novels across numerous contributors due to the different spellings. Computer catalogs have no way of knowing that "S. King" and "Stephen King" are the same person. Some common cases where contributor names may be inconsistent include:

- Initials
- Nicknames
- Pseudonyms
- Multiple surnames
- Maiden name vs married name

Disambiguation is a much bigger problem that often is harder to diagnose and correct. This problem arises when two distinct authors (or any stored contributors) have the same name. The bigger a library's catalog, the more likely this will become an issue for patron searches and overall organization. Sometimes having a different contributor role is enough to differentiate the two, but it is unwise to rely on this alone. **Assigning an international standard name identifier (ISNI) is a safe way to guarantee that two people with the same name will not be associated or confused with one another.**

CONTRIBUTOR LINKING

If "S. King" and "Stephen King" both already exist within a catalog, the undertaking to completely normalize all data points is an impossibility for some libraries. Here again, the ISNI can help ameliorate the problem by enabling linking of contributors. If the library's cataloging software allows it, this linking may be done automatically. The only important thing to remember when linking two contributors (or when linking any two data points) is to be certain that the link is accurate. Linking two different contributors will lead to inaccuracies across any other related data points.

Product Form

Product form—the format and specific binding type of a product—is critical data for libraries to make collection development decisions, and there are some common classification errors that publishers make (such as as classifying a book as "hardback" when it should actually be "library binding"). Review the ONIX list of product forms (List 150) and look for any forms that seem ambiguous to you, then research these forms to make sure you know exactly when to use them. Below are several product forms that are commonly misclassified along with information to help you make the correct classification:

"Hardback" vs "Library binding"
- Hardback: Standard hardback or cased book
- Library binding: Strengthened cloth-over-boards binding intended for libraries
    *Within ONIX, listed as a more specific product form detail (List 175)

"Audio cassette" vs "Audio tape"
- Audio cassette: Analog cassette tape
- Audio tape: Analog open reel tape

"Videodisc" vs "DVD video" vs "DVD-ROM"

- Videodisc: Laserdisc
- DVD video: Specific DVD format discs
- DVD-ROM: DVD format discs designed for use on personal computers

"Digital product license key" vs "Digital product license code"

- Digital product license key: A physical code, or "key," delivered through a retail supply chain
- Digital product license code: A digital code delivered through email or other electronic distribution

Product form details (List 175) require extra attention when assigned to a book. Several product form details listed are very closely related and should be researched thoroughly to ensure you are providing the correct ones for your physical or digital book form. ONIX generally provides a brief description of each product form and product form detail; use these to your advantage, even if you are not using ONIX, to commit to proper metadata.

GETTING EYES ON YOUR CONTENT

Perfect metadata means nothing if your content is lacking visibility. The most robust catalog in the world serves no purpose if there are no patrons utilizing it. **One key to getting patron's eyes on your content is to have your releases reviewed in leading professional journals and consumer-facing media.** Below are some of the most popular and recommended journals from which to seek reviews:

Booklist Magazine and Booklist Online

booklistonline.com

Focused primarily on public and school libraries, *Booklist*'s tagline boasts, "More than 180,000 book reviews for librarians, book groups, and book lovers—from the trusted experts at the American Library Association." *Booklist* has been around for over 100 years, starting out as a print magazine and moving onto the web in 2006.

Booklist also touts a quarterly supplement, called *Book Links*, that aims to help libraries provide kids with "high-quality literature-based resources."

Voice of Youth Advocates (VOYA)

voyamagazine.com

VOYA Magazine is a bimonthly publication started in 1978 that focuses primarily on "young adult librarians, the advocacy of young adults, and the promotion of young adult literature and reading." *VOYA* now has an established online presence and publishes a wide variety of press articles, booklists, author interviews, columns, and more. *VOYA* reviews around 350 books per issue (around 700 a month, 2,200 a year).

Publishers Weekly (PW)

publishersweekly.com

Publishers Weekly is a weekly publication aimed at a wide variety of reading audiences. The oldest publication on this list, *PW* was founded in 1860 and has evolved significantly over time. *PW*'s book reviews were not added until well into its lifetime, in 1940, but have grown significantly since. In addition to reviews, *PW* publishes a large amount of original content including news, opinion articles, and booklists.

PW also runs a website dedicated to self-publishing called BookLife. Authors and their books registered within BookLife can freely submit their writings for PW Review Consideration.

Kirkus Reviews

kirkusreviews.com

Kirkus Reviews, founded in 1933, is a bimonthly publication focused primarily on book reviews, reviewing over 7,000 books per year. In addition to editorial services, promotional services, and typical publisher review consideration submissions, *Kirkus Reviews* offers a program for independent authors to submit their books for review consideration as well.

Library Journal (LJ)

reviews.libraryjournal.com

Library Journal is directed primarily to librarians and offers a wide variety of resources, including a print and digital 20 issues-per-year publication, research materials, case studies, professional development courses, and self-publishing services (via a platform called SELF-e).

Founded in 1876, *Library Journal* is widely considered to be the most prominent librarian publication.

School Library Journal (SLJ)

slj.com

School Library Journal, as its name suggests, is a monthly publication focused on delivering reviews and other articles to a school-based educator audience. All reviews on *SLJ* are for books geared towards preschool through teens. *SLJ* also places a major emphasis on delivering news and features about technology and media, especially in how it relates to teachers and their classrooms.

School Library Journal was originally part of *Library Journal* before spinning off in 1954. *SLJ* publishes over 6,000 reviews each year.

The Horn Book

hbook.com

The Horn Book is a bimonthly publication founded in 1924 that focuses solely on books for children and young adults. In addition to more than 80,000 reviews, *The Horn Book* publishes numerous articles and features offering guidance and recommendations regarding books for young readers.

The Horn Book also offers an additional semiannual publication, *The Horn Book Guide*, that collects their reviews into a packed reader. While *The Horn Book* magazine claims to be more selective about their reviews, *The Horn Book Guide* publishes around 2,000 reviews per issue and encourages all to apply.

Bulletin of the Center for Children's Books (BCCB)

bccb.ischool.illinois.edu

The Bulletin of the Center for Children's Books, founded in 1945, is the only reviewer on this list that centers entirely on children's books. The *BCCB* is partnered closely with the Center for Children's Books, a research facility dedicated to facilitating the growth of children's education through literature. Also unlike other publications on this list, the *BCCB*'s publication and online presence focuses exclusively on reviews, with no other content like blog posts or news articles.

The application process to submit your books for review is relatively similar across all publications listed above. While some recommend signing up for their exclusive self-publishing programs that generally offer an advantage in the submission process, all provide some other avenue of submission for consideration on their websites. Take a look at each of the publications and submit to one or more where your book seems to be a good fit.

TAKEAWAYS

Using metadata to get the most out of a library's catalog is important. With utilizing book review channels and getting your content's complexity levels rated and sorted for use in reading programs, there is a lot of work to be done to guarantee maximum coverage for each release.

At the core is your metadata. Going beyond simple things like title and author, your book's final presentation to patrons is the sum of its parts, and if those parts are incomplete or inaccurate, everything will crumble.

We hope that we have been helpful in outlining the following:

- Outlined essential metadata focus points for library-specific issues

- Explained reading complexity scoring and summarized some prominent reading programs

- Informed you of prominent book review publications and their review and submission histories

Taking the information here to heart is a fantastic first step to improve your metadata. We feel that combining this knowledge with other sections found in this book will help you to solve pain points in your data that are causing headaches in cataloging and discoverability.

GLOSSARY

Affiliations Connects a contributor to corporations, organizations, or institutions they belong to.

Age range Utilized for children and young adult titles to specify the exact age range in years or grade level of the intended audience for a product.

Attribute A piece of metadata that describes a book such as a subject code or a contributor name.

Audience code Identifies the broad audience or readership for a product.

BIC category Subject classification used mainly within the UK book trade and some other English language markets.

BISAC regional theme code Used in conjunction with BISAC subject codes, these codes help to identify titles with a strong relationship to a geographic region.

BISAC subject code Subject classification for use in the U.S. and English-speaking Canada. Used to guide shelving, categorization, merchandising, and marketing.

Comp titles Also known as readalikes, these are examples of previously published books that are similar to a title.

Contributor bio Biographical note about a title's author.

Contributor place relator Information about where the author was born, died, currently lives, formerly lived, etc.

Contributor role The function of each individual who took part in the creation of a title.

Country of origin The single country where a product was originally developed and/or published.

Dimensions The length, depth, width, and height measurements of a title.

Edition Used to specify a book's revision and re-release into an existing or new marketplace.

Edition description A short, concise statement that accurately and purposefully combines the edition number and edition type.

Enhanced metadata Richer marketing-related metadata to help sell the book, such as: author bios, promotional information, keywords, and reviews.

Glossary Usually found at the end of a book, this is an alphabetical list of names and/or subjects within the content and a description of each.

HTML markup Symbols or codes used to help format text on site. (e.g. use <b> for bold, <i> for italics and <p> for paragraph breaks)

Index Usually found at the end of a book, this is an alphabetical list of names and/or subjects with a reference to where they can be found within the book.

Indexing, search engine The practice of collecting and storing data for search on a site or search engine.

Interest age Specifies age range for higher-level books that appeal to an older audience.

Machine learning A type of artificial intelligence (AI) that allows software applications to become more accurate in predicting outcomes without being explicitly programmed.

Measure type Contains the physical measurements for the height, width, weight and other aspects of a physical book.

Measure unit Specifies the unit of measurement (grams, inches, centimeters, etc.) for the measure type.

Metadata Information that describes and provides information about other data.

Features Additional description of the product format. (e.g. accessibility features for print-impaired readers)

ISNI International Standard Name Identifier, a unique code used to help link and distinguish individual contributors.

Keywords Additional topics, categories, and consumer search terms related to the book.

Product description Often referred to as the "elevator pitch" for your title, this is detailed descriptive copy appropriate for public display, used for marketing, discovery, and sales purposes.

Product form The primary means of distinguishing between different version of the same intellectual work. (e.g. hardcover, trade paperback, mass-market paperback, and audio)

Product form detail Used in conjunction with the product form code, this is an additional level of detail to describe the type of book. (e.g. coloring book, miniature book, and picture book)

Reading levels Complexity level of the content for any juvenile titles with appeal to the educational market (in the form of a Lexile measure or other leveling standard).

Related product Products similar or related to the main product.

Relational algorithms Used by retailers to determine related products. (e.g. titles by the same author)

Review quotes Praise or informational quotes from published reviews for the title and/or contributor(s). Ideally, reviews will come from people and publications known by and influential with potential buyers.

SEO Search engine optimization. The practice of creating and modifying web content and metadata to increase your rankings in search results.

Series name Specific name of a theme-, character-, or plot-driven grouping of titles.

Series number For a numbered series, the series number specifies the ordered place (number) of the title in the series.

Short description Brief description appropriate for public display, used for marketing, discovery, and sales purposes.

Subtitle A secondary, often descriptive or explanatory title for the book.

Title The primary title of the book as it appears on the title page.

Territory rights Publisher-chosen publication rights for specified geographical territories.

Thema code Multilingual subject classification for use worldwide.

Weight Measure of the individual weight for physical products.

INDEX

9 781513 260891